RALPH S... hiked an... Sassenach by birth, he has lived in S... at Dundee University and has a grea... he can be seen in all weathers roam... tops. As well as disappearing into the .... or nature, he also writes novels and sexological non-fiction, and produces dark-wave music on his home computer.

Baffies' Easy Munro Guide, Volume 2: Central Highlands is the second ...... a series that draws on his decades of experience in finding ...... up the Scottish mountains.

...... or *Baffies' Easy Munro Guide, Volume 1: Southern Highlands*

...... the covers of this slim volume is a truly outstanding guidebook
...OVERED SCOTLAND

...... e for his complementary series *The Ultimate Guide to the Munros*

...... a truly indispensible guide for the Munro-bagger. Bursting with ...ation, wit and a delightful irreverence rarely found in this type ...le, it's a joy to read. Ralph and his motley crew are the perfect ...nions on a great day out. An absolute gem! ALEX MacKINNON, ...r. Waterstone's George Street, Edinburgh

...ate Guide to The Munros *picks up where others – including* ...*– leave off, with lots of nitty-gritty information on alternative* ...*levels of difficulty and aids to navigation, all in a very up-beat* ...*look forward to seeing the rest of his fun-packed Munros* ...AMERON MCNEISH

Cultu
& Spo

...sly illustrated...Entertaining as well as informative... One of the ...e guides to the Munros. PRESS & JOURNAL

Irresistibly funny and useful; an innovatively thought-through guide-book that makes an appetising broth of its wit, experience and visual and literary tools. Brilliant. OUTDOOR WRITERS & PHOTOGRAPHERS GUILD

After much praise and cult following from avid Munro baggers following the first book comes the second volume in The Ultimate Guide to the Munros *series... Ralph Storer preserves the quirky charm that made the first book a loveable essential for hill walkers... the book is as fun as it is practical...* EDINBURGH EVENING NEWS

While most climbing authors appear to have had their funny bones surgically removed, Storer is happy to share numerous irreverent insights into the hills, and this acts as a timely reminder that walking should, after all, be primarily about enjoyment of the great outdoors. SCOTTISH FIELD

With the winning combination of reliable advice and quirky humour, this is the ideal hillwalking companion. SCOTS MAGAZINE

His books are exceptional... Storer subverts the guidebook genre completely. THE ANGRY CORRIE

BY THE SAME AUTHOR:

100 Best Routes on Scottish Mountains (Little Brown)
50 Best Routes on Skye and Raasay (Birlinn)
50 Classic Routes on Scottish Mountains (Luath Press)
Exploring Scottish Hill Tracks (Little Brown)
The Joy of Hillwalking (Luath Press)

The Ultimate Guide to the Munros series:
    Volume 1: Southern Highlands
    Volume 2: Central Highlands South (including Glen Coe)
    Volume 3: Central Highlands North (including Ben Nevis)

Also in *Baffies' Easy Munro Guide* series:
    Volume 1: Southern Highlands

Baffies' Easy Munro Guide

Volume 2: Central Highlands including Ben Nevis and Glen Coe

RALPH STORER

Boot-tested and compiled by
Baffies, Entertainments Convenor
The Go-Take-a-Hike Mountaineering Club

Luath Press Limited

EDINBURGH

www.luath.co.uk

For Toni

First published 2012

ISBN: 978-1-908373-20-5

Printed and bound by Bell and Bain Ltd., Glasgow

Typeset in Tahoma by Ralph Storer

All maps reproduced by permission of Ordnance Survey on behalf of HMSO.
© Crown copyright 2010. All rights reserved. Ordnance Survey Licence number
100016659.

All photographs by the author.

CONTENTS

PREFACE

So you want to climb Munros but have understandable concerns that you may end up teetering precariously above an abysmal drop, sitting gingerly astride a knife-edge ridge or groping futilely for handfuls of grass on a crumbling rock ledge. If possible, you'd like to make it down to the foot of the mountain again. In one piece. Before dusk.

Let me introduce you to your new best friend: Baffies, the Entertainments Convenor of the Go-Take-a-Hike Mountaineering Club. In his club bio he lists himself as someone who is allergic to exertion, is prone to lassitude, suffers from altitude sickness above 600m, blisters easily and bleeds readily. However meagre your hillwalking credentials, if he can make it to the summit, so can you.

Our sister publication *The Ultimate Guide to the Munros* does what it says on the cover and describes routes of *all* kinds up *all* of the Munros. Not *all* of these are suitable for sensitive souls such as Baffies, hence the decision to 'delegate' him to write the guidebook you now hold in your hands.

When the club committee first suggested to him that he was the ideal person for the task, he almost choked on his triple chocolate layer cake. Only after we had managed to hold him down long enough to explain the book's remit did he come to embrace the idea. Indeed, he set about researching the contents with such a hitherto unseen fervour and thoroughness that we are proud to have the results associated with the club's name – a guidebook dedicated to finding easy ways up Munros.

Herein you will find easy walking routes up 25 Munros (and more!) – routes that require no rock climbing, no scrambling, no tightrope walking, no technical expertise whatsoever. Of course, hillwalking can never be a risk-free activity. No Munro is as easy to reach from an armchair as is the TV remote. You will be expected to be able to put one foot in front of the other... and repeat.

Given that proviso, you will find no easier way to climb Munros than to follow in the footsteps of Baffies. I leave you in his capable hands.

Ralph Storer, President
Go-Take-a-Hike Mountaineering Club

INTRODUCTION

OF MOUNTAINS AND MUNROS

It's a big place, the Scottish Highlands. It contains so many mountains that even resident hillwalkers struggle to climb them all in a lifetime. How many mountains? That depends...

If two summits 100m apart are separated by a shallow dip, do they constitute two mountains or one mountain with two tops? If the latter, then exactly how far apart do they have to be, and how deep does the intervening dip have to be, before they become two separate mountains?

Sir Hugh Munro (1856–1919), the third President of the Scottish Mountaineering Club, tackled this problem when he published his 'Tables of Heights over 3000 Feet' in the 1891 edition of the SMC Journal. Choosing the criterion of 3000ft in the imperial system of measurement as his cut-off point, he counted 283 separate Mountains and a further 255 Tops that were over 3000ft but not sufficiently separated from a Mountain to be considered separate Mountains themselves.

In a country whose vertical axis ranges from 0ft to 4409ft (1344m) at the summit of Ben Nevis, the choice of 3000ft as a cut-off point is aesthetically justifiable and gives a satisfying number of Mountains. A metric cut-off point of 1000m (3280ft), giving a more humble 137 Mountains, has never captured the hillgoing imagination.

Unfortunately Sir Hugh omitted to leave to posterity the criteria he used to distinguish Mountains from Tops, and Tops from other highpoints over 3000ft. In his notes to the Tables he even broached the impossibility of ever making definitive distinctions. Consider, for example, the problem of differentiating between Mountains, Tops and other highpoints on the

BINNEIN MOR

Sir Hugh Munro himself never became a Munroist (someone who has climbed all the Munros). Of the Tables of the day, he climbed all but three: the Inaccessible Pinnacle (although that did not become a Munro until 1921), Carn an Fhidhleir and Carn Cloich-mhuilinn. The latter, which he was saving until last because it was close to his home, was ironically demoted to Top status in 1981.

Cairngorm plateaus, where every knoll surpasses 3000ft.

The Tables were a substantial achievement in an age when mapping of the Highlands was still rudimentary, but no sooner did they appear than their definitiveness become the subject of debate. In subsequent years Munro continued to fine-tune them, using new sources such as the Revised Six-inch Survey of the late 1890s. His notes formed the basis of a new edition of the Tables, published posthumously in 1921, which listed 276 separate Mountains (now known as Munros) and 267 Tops.

The 1921 edition also included J. Rooke Corbett's list of mountains with heights between 2500ft and 3000ft ('Corbetts'), and Percy Donald's list of hills in the Scottish Lowlands of 2000ft or over ('Donalds'). Corbett's test for a separate mountain was that it needed a re-ascent of 500ft (c150m) on all sides. Donald's test was more mathematical. A 'Donald' had to be 17 units from another one, where a unit was one twelfth of a mile (approx. one seventh of a kilometre) or one 50ft (approx. 15m) contour. We can assume that, however informally, Munro used some similar formula concerning distance and height differential.

Over the years, various developments have conspired to prompt further amendments to the Tables, including metrication, improved surveying methods (most recently by satellite), and a desire on the part of each succeeding generation of editors to reduce what they have regarded as 'anomalies.' For example, the 'mountain range in miniature' of Beinn Eighe was awarded a second Munro in 1997 to redress the balance with similar but over-endowed multi-topped ridges such as the seven-Munro South Glen Shiel Ridge. Changes and the reasons for change are detailed individually in the main text (see Peak Fitness for details).

The first metric edition of the Tables in 1974 listed 279 Munros and 262 Tops. The 1981 edition listed 276 Munros and 240 Tops. The 1990 edition added an extra Munro. The latest (1997) edition lists 284 Munros and 227 Tops, but Sgurr nan Ceannaichean was demoted to Corbett status following re-measurement in 2009, leaving 283. Watch this space.

The first person to bag all the Munros may have been the Rev Archibald Robertson in 1901, although his notebooks bear no mention of him having climbed the Inaccessible Pinnacle and note that he gave up on Ben Wyvis to avoid a wetting.

The second Munroist was the Rev Ronald Burn, who additionally bagged all the Tops, in 1923, thus becoming the first 'Compleat Munroist' or Compleater. The third was James Parker, who additionally bagged all the Tops and Furths (the 3000ft summits of England, Wales and Ireland), in 1929. The latest edition of the Tables lists 1745 known Munroists.

THE SCOTTISH HIGHLANDS

The Scottish Highlands are characterised by a patchwork of mountains separated by deep glens, the result of glacial erosion in the distant past. On a global scale the mountains reach an insignificant height, topping out at (1344m/4409ft) on Ben Nevis. But in form they hold their own against any range in the world, many rising bold and beautiful from sea-level. For hillwalkers they have distinct advantages over higher mountain ranges: their height is ideal for day walks and glens give easy road access.

Moreover, the variety of mountain forms and landscapes is arguably greater than in any mountainous area of equivalent size. This is due to many factors, notably differing regional geology and the influence of the sea.

In an attempt to give some order to this complexity, the Highlands are traditionally divided into six regions, as detailed below. The potted overviews mislead in that they mask the variety within each region, ignore numerous exceptions to the rule and reflect road access as much as discernible regional boundaries, but they serve as introductory descriptions.

On Sgairneach Mhor

The Southern Highlands 46 Munros	Gentle, green and accessible, with scope for a great variety of mountain walks.
The Central Highlands 73 Munros	A combination of all the other regions, with some of the greatest rock faces in the country.
The Cairngorms 50 Munros	Great rolling plateaus, vast corries, remote mountain sanctuaries, sub-arctic ambience.
The Western Highlands 63 Munros	Dramatic landscapes, endless seascapes, narrow ridges, arrowhead peaks, rugged terrain.
The Northern Highlands 39 Munros	Massive, monolithic mountains rising out of a desolate, watery wilderness.
The Islands 13 Munros	Exquisite mountainscapes, knife-edge ridges, sky-high scrambling, maritime ambience.

THE CENTRAL HIGHLANDS

The Central Highlands form the smallest of the six regions of the Scottish Highlands and Islands, yet they are packed with more Munros and a greater variety of scenery than any of the other five.

On the north and west the region is bounded by the great fault line that runs through Loch Linnhe and continues up the Great Glen from Fort William to Inverness. On the east it is bounded by the A9, which runs north from Perth over Drumochter Pass to Aviemore and Inverness. The southern boundary runs along the A85 from Oban to Tyndrum, up the A82 to Rannoch Moor, then east beside Lochs Rannoch and Tummel to Pitlochry.

From Scotland's populous Central Belt, two main arteries lead north and west through the region. From Dalwhinnie on the A9, the A86 runs west along Loch Laggan through Glen Spean to Spean Bridge and Fort William, at the entrance to Glen Nevis. From Crianlarich, where the Edinburgh and Glasgow roads meet, the A82 runs west to Tyndrum, then north-west through Bridge of Orchy and across the edge of Rannoch Moor to Glen Etive and Glen Coe.

As you travel along the roads, you'll be aware of a changing landscape that reflects a varied underlying geology, from the granite of Ben Cruachan in the south to the mica-schist of the Monadh Liath in the north, from the sandstones of Loch Ericht in the east to the quartzite of the Mamores and Grey Corries in the west.

The Mamores from Ben Nevis

Let's get one thing straight: taking the easy way up a Munro does not diminish your hillwalking credentials. Just because you have your mind set on higher matters than groping rock all day doesn't mean you have to hang up your boots and go lie on a beach. The joys of hillwalking are not circumscribed by the difficulty of the endeavour. Sir Hugh himself was perfectly happy to take an easy way up a mountain if there was one and there's no reason you shouldn't follow in his footsteps.

Erupting through this geological base, volcanic extrusions have created the most dramatic scenery of all around Glen Coe and Ben Nevis, the highest mountain in the land. Fault lines and depressions, often paralleling the Highland Boundary Fault to the south, further divide the region into mountain groups, and yet more sculpting of the landscape occurred during Ice Ages.

The end-result is a region of rugged scenery and stark contrasts, but one in which complexity of landscape still leaves room for individual Munros of great presence, be they characterised by the jagged ridges of the west, the rolling plateaus of the east or the remote summits of the roadless hinterland in-between. Whatever your taste in mountain scenery, there is something here for everyone.

The region contains no less than 73 Munros, to say nothing of 64 accompanying Tops and 35 Corbetts. But of course not all of them are easy to climb. Some of them are so far from a roadside that they are practically out of reach as day walks using a car, while others are difficult to climb without scrambling up rock.

Of the 73 Munros shown on the maps on the following pages, this guidebook describes easy routes up 25 of them (marked R1–R25), selected to showcase a cross-section of Central Highlands geography and mountain form. They are described in roughly west-to-east and south-to-north order.

If you reach all the summits you will come to know the Central Highlands intimately… and perhaps want to explore some of the more demanding Munros described in our sister series: *The Ultimate Guide to the Munros.*

Memo to self: What are you waiting for? Get your boots on!

On Beinn a' Chochuill summit ridge in winter

BEINN EUNAICH

BEINN A' CHOCHUILL

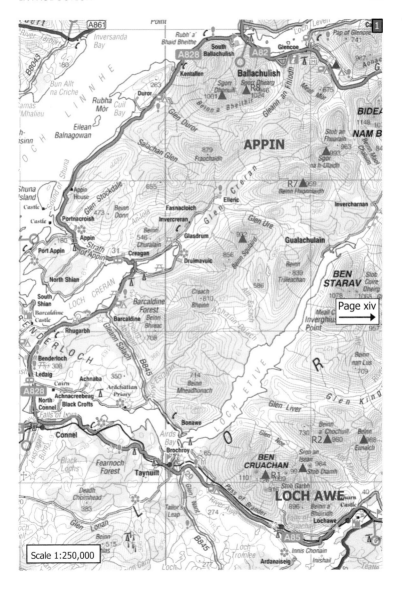

Scale 1:250,000

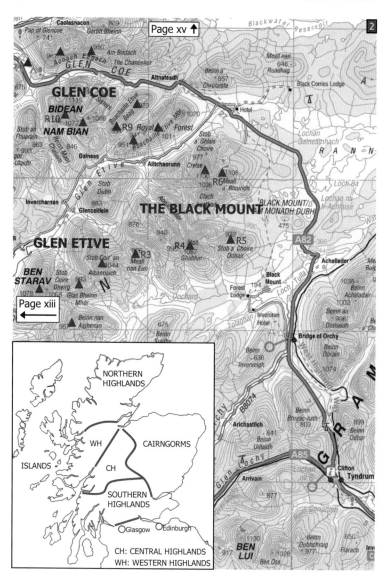

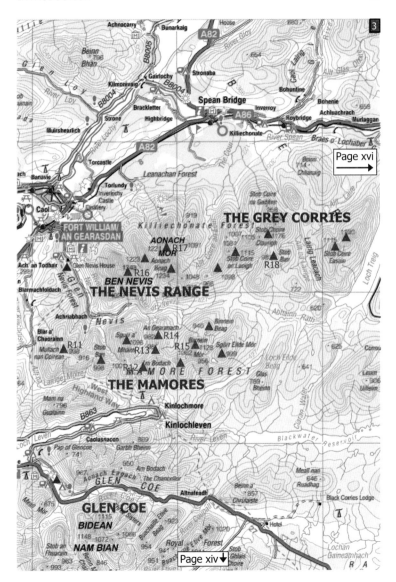

Page xvi →

Page xiv ↓

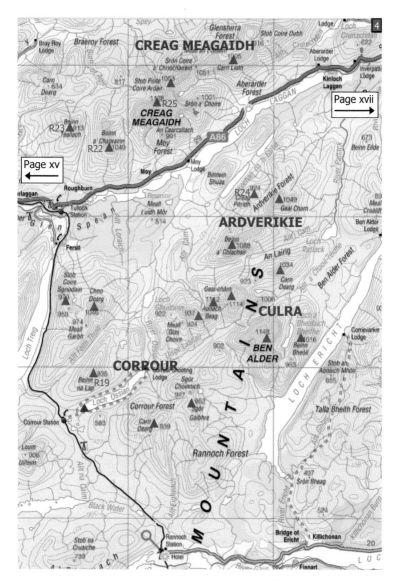

Page xvii →

← Page xv

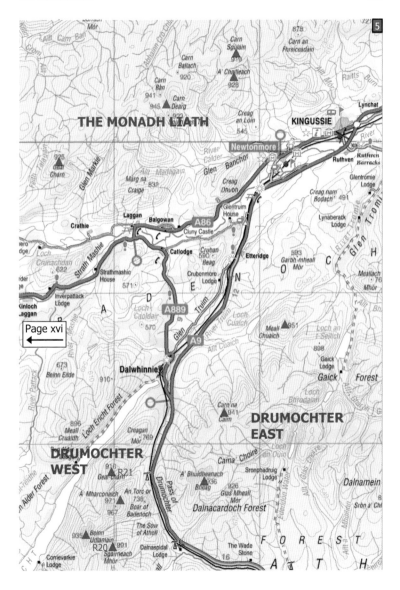

Page xvi ←

SEASONS AND WEATHER

From a hillwalking perspective, the Highland year has two seasons: the snow season and the no-snow season. The length of these seasons varies from year to year and from place to place.

From May to September, snow is rarely a problem. Historically, May and June have the greatest number of sunny days, with the air at its clearest. July and August are the hottest months but are also more prone to rain and haze, not to mention that blight on the landscape, the Highland midge. The biting season begins in mid to late June and lasts until the first chills of late September. By October it is colder, the hills get their first dusting of winter snow and good days are few and far between.

The months from November to April, though sometimes earlier and later, are characterised by short days, cold and snow. March and April are transition months, with little or lots of snow. In some years, snow can last into early summer and be a nuisance on some routes. If you are unequipped for it, turn back. Snow is more treacherous to descend than ascend, and spring snow often has a crystalline quality that makes it behave like ball-bearings.

In a normal winter (whatever that is, these days), conditions vary from British to Alpine to Arctic. An easy summer route can be made life-threatening by icy conditions and severe winter weather. When paths are obliterated by snow, hillsides become treacherous and walking becomes difficult and tiring.

On a clear winter's day the Scottish mountains have an Alpine quality that makes for unforgettable days out, but no-one should attempt a Munro in winter without adequate clothing and equipment (including ice-axe and crampons), and experience (or the company of an experienced person). The number of accidents, some of them fatal, that occur in the Highlands every winter should leave no doubt as to the need for caution.

BUACHAILLE ETIVE BEAG

Sample weather forecasts:
www.metoffice.gov.uk/loutdoor/
    mountainsafety/ Tel: West (09068-
    500442), East (09068-500441))
www.metcheck.com/V40/UK/HOBBIES/
    mountain.asp   www.mwis.org.uk
www.sais.gov.uk (avalanche conditions)

Useful webcams at the time of writing
can be found at:
    www.kingy.com
    www.glencoemountain.com
    www.nevisrange.co.uk/
    visit-fortwilliam.co.uk/webcam/
    trafficscotland.org/lev/

USING THIS BOOK

Position in Munro's Tables
(1 = highest)

OS 1:50,000
map number

Grid reference

▲**Ben Cruachan** **31** 1126m/3694ft (OS 50, NN 069304)
Ben Croo-achan, Mountain of Mounds

Many Munro names are Gaelic in origin. We give approximate pronunciations but make no claim to definitiveness. For example, the correct pronunciation of Ben is akin to *Pyne*, with a soft *n* as in the first syllable of *onion*, but it would be pedantic to enforce a purist pronunciation on a non-Gaelic speaker. The name Bealach, meaning Pass, is pronounced *byalach*, but many find it

hard not to call it a *beelach*. And if you're one of those unfortunates who appear congenitally incapable of pronouncing *loch* as anything other than *lock*, you're in trouble.

In connection with the phonetic pronunciations given, note that Y before a vowel is pronounced as in *you*, OW is pronounced as in *town* and CH is pronounced as in Scottish *loch* or German *noch*.

Stob Ban from Coirechoille (Glen Spean)
NN 256788, 11ml/17km, 850m/2800ft

The maps used in this book are reproductions of OS 1:50,000 maps at 75% full size (i.e. 1:66,667 or 1.5cm per 1km).

Route distances are specified in miles (to the nearest half-mile) and kilometres (to the nearest kilometre). Short distances are specified in metres (an approximate imperial measurement is yards). Total amount of ascent for a route is specified to the nearest 10m (50ft) and should be regarded as an approximation only.

To calculate how long a route will take, many begin with Naismith's Rule (one hour per 3ml/5km + half-hour

per 1000ft/300m). This can be adjusted by an appropriate factor to suit your own pace and to cater for stoppages, foul weather, technical difficulty, rough terrain, tiredness and decrepitude. (Bill Naismith, 1856–1935, was the 'father' of the SMC.)

River directions, left bank and right bank, refer to the downstream direction. When referring to the direction of travel, we specify left-hand and right-hand.

The symbols ▲ and Δ indicate Munros and Tops. An ATV track is an All-Terrain Vehicle track, rougher than a Land Rover track.

ACCESS

Land access was revolutionised by The Land Reform (Scotland) Act 2003 and the accompanying Scottish Outdoor Access Code (2005), which created a statutory right of responsible access for outdoor recreation. It is recommended that anyone walking in the Scottish countryside familiarise himself/herself with the Code, which explains rights and responsibilities in detail. Further information: www.outdooraccess-scotland.com.

Deer stalking considerations: Most of the Scottish Highlands are privately owned and non-compliance with stalking restrictions is likely to cause aggravation for all concerned. If revenue is lost because of interference with stalking activities, estates may be forced to turn to afforestation or worse, thereby increasing access problems.

The red stag stalking season runs from July 1 to October 20 but actual dates vary from locality to locality. Access notices dot the roadside and information on stalking activities can be obtained from estate offices and head stalkers. Specific information given in the main text is subject to change and should be verified.

An increasing number of estates contribute to the Hillphones service, which provides daily recorded messages of where stalking is taking place. Further information can be found on the Outdoor Access website or on the Hillphones website: www.hillphones.info. Alternatively, leaflets can be obtained from The Mountaineering Council of Scotland, The Old Granary, Perth PH1 5QP.

Note that there is no stalking on a Sunday and that access to land owned by public bodies such as the Forestry Commission, the National Trust for Scotland and the John Muir Trust is normally not subject to restriction.

TERRAIN

There are boot-worn paths on most of the standard ascent routes, but don't expect the kind of manufactured paths to be found in the Alps, Rockies or even the Furth of Scotland (England and Wales). Boggy ground is commonplace, and in some cases rugged terrain precludes the formation of a path at all.

On the more popular routes, path restoration continues apace. The boggy morass of the former Coire Ardair path, for instance, is now a beautiful approach route. In general, however, be prepared always for rough, rugged terrain and wear appropriate footwear.

BEN NEVIS Mountain Track

▲Ben Cruachan 31 1126m/3694ft (OS 50, NN 069304) *Ben Croo-achan*, Mountain of Mounds

Stob Dearg | BEN CRUACHAN | Drochaid Ghlas
Meall Cuanail
Coire Cruachan
dam
Loch Awe

The close-knit mountain mass that crowds Loch Awe's north shore might be expected to sprawl ignominiously in all directions, but the Cruachan Range eschews such preconceptions. Its two Munros and five Tops are all shapely affairs that have narrow ridges to spare.

The slimline topography is due to deep corries that have been glacially hollowed out of the massif's flanks to both north and south. There are four craggy little corries on the remote north side and one humungous basin on the south side – Coire Cruachan.

More remarkable even than the range's ice-sculpted shapeliness, considering the chance mountain-building activities that have brought it about, is the striking symmetry of Coire Cruachan's architecture. Its east and west bounding ridges rise to the two Munros — Ben Cruachan itself and Stob Diamh (*Stop Daff*, Stag Peak). These are linked by a narrow, rocky connecting ridge around the north side of the corrie.

Of the five additional Tops, one lies between the two Munros, two form southern outposts on each side of the corrie, and two lie to east and west, outwith the corrie skyline.

The Cruachan Horseshoe, as the round of the corrie skyline is known, is an adventurous scramble, but the reigning peak is more easily reached from the bowl of the corrie by the route described here. Stob Diamh too is an easy separate objective from the corrie on another day (see Page 5).

Ben Cruachan from Loch Awe
NN 078268, 6ml/10km, 1080m/3550ft

Ben Cruachan takes pride of place in this guidebook both geographically and symbolically, as though the Central Highlands were anxious to advertise their wares right from the start.

Paths into Coire Cruachan climb each side of the Allt Cruachan directly from the A85 Lochaweside road. The east-side (right-hand) path is the main approach path, while the rougher west-side (left-hand) path is a possible descent option. As the starting point is only c.40m/130ft above sea-level, the height gain to the summit of

Ben Cruachan is greater than on any Munro outside the Nevis Range. We thought you'd like to know that.

The east-side path begins 200m east of Cruachan power station, opposite Falls of Cruachan railway halt. Park on the roadside verge as the nearby Visitor Centre allows only two hours parking.

Start up the flight of concrete steps leading to the station, leave the path at the first corner to go through a gate and under the railway line, then climb more steps to hydro works. Just before the steps end, the east-side path goes

BEN CRUACHAN

Coire Dearg

Coire Cruachan

Cruachan Reservoir

Not only has Ben Cruachan been hollowed out by ice, but it is *literally* hollow, in that the hydro-electric works fed by Cruachan Reservoir, which fills Coire Cruachan, are located in great underground caverns. The dimensions of the machine hall indicate the scale of the enterprise: 90m/300ft long by 23m/77ft wide by 36m/120ft high.

left through the trees to climb beside the Allt Cruachan. It is hemmed in by thick undergrowth but is well drained and in a fair state. It's a 360m/1200ft climb to the reservoir and height is gained fast (i.e. it's steep).

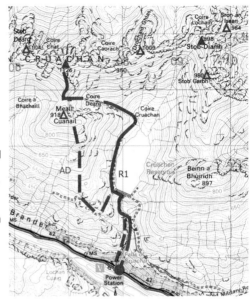

In the wooded gorge of the Allt Cruachan you'll hear but won't see the hidden Falls of Cruachan, now reduced in volume by the hydro scheme. Above the gorge the path levels off before climbing more gently into Coire Cruachan, with a first glimpse of the summit of Ben Cruachan above the dam.

When the path reaches the dam access road, follow it left across a bridge to the dam foot, then zigzag up grassy steps and climb a metal ladder beside the concrete wall. You emerge atop the dam for a first view of the reservoir backed by the skyline.

From the near left-hand corner of the dam, a path takes a short-cut to an unpaved road. Follow this along the west side of the reservoir to the foot of the stream that comes down from the Bealach an Lochain (Pass of the Lochan, unnamed on OS map).

This is the bealach south of Ben Cruachan between the summit and the Top of Meall Cuanail (*Meall Coo-anil*, Hill of the Flocks), which is only 90m/300ft higher than the bealach. A path up to the bealach begins at a roadside cairn 100m before the road-end.

The path is boggy at first as it traverses the

BEN CRUACHAN

Meall Cuanail

Coire Dearg

Stob Garbh

hillside to the stream. It then crosses the stream to the right-hand bank and follows it all the way up to the bealach. It becomes drier as it enters the bowl of Coire Dearg and is very pleasant for a while on rock-strewn grass slopes. At the back of the corrie it becomes steeper and stonier as it climbs into a tiny upper corrie and then to the bealach, where there is a large cairn and a small pond.

There is no respite as the stony path turns right and continues up the steep, shattered slopes of Ben Cruachan's south ridge. After an initial scree-like section, the ridge becomes more well-defined, with better going for a while on grass and boulders, but then you reach the foot of the final boulder pile and from hereon you'll be lucky to stay

Bealach
an Lochain

Coire
Dearg

BEN CRUACHAN

STOB DIAMH →

Bealach an Lochain

upright. The path stays left, seeking firmer going among whatever patches of grass it can find.

The small ▲summit area is festooned with big granite boulders, such that the cairn isn't quite the highest point. No less than four steep ridges meet here, giving a sensation of great height and affording an immense summit view.

With a length of almost 25ml/40km, Loch Awe is the longest loch in Scotland, being more than a mile longer than Loch Ness and almost three miles longer than Loch Lomond. Unlike that more famous loch, which narrows beneath Ben Lomond, Loch Awe broadens when its north end is blocked by Ben Cruachan.

The loch is also remarkable in that its inlet and outlet have been reversed by Ice Age activity. The outlet used to be to the south, until glacial pressure forced a way through the Pass of Brander beneath Cruachan and excavated a northern outlet.

Add a number of historic islands, complete with castles and churches, and you have one interesting loch to study as you stride its surrounding mountains.

BEN CRUACHAN

Drochaid Ghlas

Viewed across Coire Cruachan from Stob Garbh

If you still have adventure in your legs after your exertions on high, consider descending from the dam by the path on the west side of the Allt Cruachan, which reaches the A85 opposite the power station, a short distance from the start of the route. It's rough, it's steep and in places it even tunnels through undergrowth, but it maximises evening views over the island-studded northern reaches of Loch Awe. It descends to the railway line, crosses it and joins a short track down to the roadside.

Alternative Descent: Meall Cuanail add-on 90m/300ft

From the Bealach an Lochain a path left of an old fence makes the short climb to Cuanail's Δsummit, which is a great viewpoint above Loch Awe. Still following the line of the fence, the path continues down the broad, boulder-strewn grass slopes of Cuanail's south-west ridge towards the reservoir dam.

The hillside above the dam is beset with crags, so stay high until beyond them, following the crest of the ridge down to a hydro road at its foot. Then wander down the road to the dam.

From the dam Stob Diamh is as easy to reach as Ben Cruachan. A path runs along the east side of the reservoir and climbs towards the skyline. When it peters out , bear left up grass slopes and continue across ΔStob Garbh (*Stob Garrav*, Rough Peak).

STOB DIAMH

Stob Garbh

Cruachan Reservoir

To see *inside* Ben Cruachan, take the guided tour from the Visitor Centre, located next to the power station near the start of the route. And there's a café too.
  Opening hours: 9.30-5.00 daily from Easter to end of October, 10.00-4.00 Monday-Friday November to mid-December and February/March, closed mid-December to late January. Tel: 01866-822618. Website: www.visitcruachan.co.uk.

▲Beinn a' Chochuill 172 980m/3215ft (OS 50, NN 109328)
Ben a Chochill, Mountain of the Cowl or Hood

BEINN A' CHOCHUILL

BEINN EUNAICH

Kilchurn Castle

Loch Awe

Beinn a' Chochuill stands half-hidden and half-forgotten behind the more eye-catching peaks of the Cruachan Range. It's worth a closer look. While its sweeping grassy slopes sport nothing to distract attention from its showier neighbour, its summit environs offer carefree and viewsome hillwalking, Sound-of-Music-style.

It is connected to the bulkier Munro of Beinn Eunaich (*Ben Ennich*, Fowling Mountain) by a 728m/2390ft bealach called the Lairig Lanachain. You could climb both Munros together, but Eunaich's steeper slopes are tougher to negotiate, especially on descent at the end of the day (see Page 9).

Beinn a' Chochuill is a more elegant mountain, consisting almost entirely of a long, sinuous east-west ridge that that gives unsurpassed views of Ben Cruachan's craggy northern corries.

Kilchurn Castle stands on a peninsula, once an island, at the north-east corner of Loch Awe. It was constructed by Campbell clan chiefs over a number of centuries. The five-storey tower dates back to the mid-fifteenth century.

The castle was garrisoned by government troops during the 1715 and 1745 Jacobite uprisings and was finally abandoned after being struck by lightning in 1760.

Open April to September. Access from A85 roadside under the nearby railway viaduct, c.400m from the A819 junction.

Beinn a' Chochuill from Loch Awe
NN 136288, 7ml/11km, 930m/3050ft

The route begins at the bridge over the Allt Mhoille (*Owlt Vull-ya*, Slow Stream) on the B8077 at the north-east corner of Loch Awe. Park with consideration on the roadside verge on the west side of the

bridge and take the farm track leading to Castles Farm on the east side. Keep left at an immediate fork, then left again when nearing the farm, to follow a hydro track up the broad glen of the Allt Mhoille.

BEINN A' CHOCHUILL

SW Spur

Lairig Noe

SE Spur

The track rises steadily across Beinn Eunaich's grassy western hillside. Staying high above the river, it aims straight for Beinn a' Chochuill ahead, giving a speedy approach route with excellent views to the left of the peaks

BEN CRUACHAN   The view from the SE Spur in winter

Lairig Noe

of the Cruachan Range.

After descending slightly to cross the Allt Lairig Lanachain, the track climbs to a junction at a height of nearly 400m/1300ft. Immediately above here rises your highway to the skyline – Beinn a' Chochuill's south-east spur.

Ignore the left branch of the track, which climbs towards the Lairig Noe between Beinn a' Chochuill and Stob Diamh, and take the right branch, which climbs 50m/150ft to a small dam on a side stream that flows down from a shallow corrie. The south-east spur is the left-hand rim of this corrie.

The grassy hillside is quite broad at first, which enables you to begin climbing it anywhere between the track junction and the dam, as you think fit. As the spur becomes more well-defined, lines of approach merge to form a good path on the crest. The ascent is fairly relentless but the path and good grassy going enable height to be gained fast.

The spur eases off as it tops out on the crest of Beinn a' Chochuill's east ridge. You reach the skyline at a small dip between two minor rises (NN 118325), about halfway up from the Lairig Lanachain.

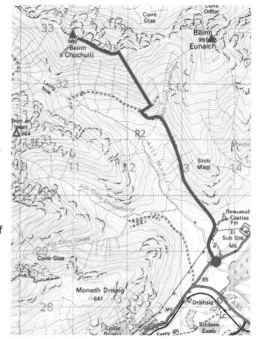

STOB DIAMH   BEN CRUACHAN   BEINN A' CHOCHUILL

Lairig Lanachain

Viewed from Beinn Eunaich

After a short climb to a rocky hump, the ridge swings right across a gently undulating section. The path wends its way amiably over grass and boulders, giving such wonderful walking that it is a pity it doesn't go on for longer. A final, steeper slope puts you atop the small ▲summit plateau, close to the edge of northern crags.

BEINN A' CHOCHUILL summit ridge

See also picture on Page xii

From the summit of Beinn a Chochuill it is possible to make a round trip by going down the south-west spur, the only other weakness on this side of the mountain, to the Lairig Noe. However, this is much steeper than the south-east spur and the grassy slopes that continue down from the lairig to the left branch of the hydro track are very marshy. Not recommended.

At the foot of Beinn a' Chochuill's east ridge steeper, rockier slopes climb from the Lairig Lanachain to the summit of Beinn Eunaich. A path picks a way up without fuss and continues down the south ridge, back towards Loch Awe, but the final descent to the approach track, avoiding the crags of Stob Maol, is very steep and stony.

BEINN EUNAICH

S Ridge

Lairig
Lanachain

BEINN A' CHOCHUILL

▲Meall nan Eun 254 928m/3045ft (OS 50, NN 192449)
Myowl nan Ee-an, Hill of the Birds

STOB COIR' AN ALBANNAICH

MEALL NAN EUN

Meall Tarsuinn

Loch Dochard

Viewed from the east

North of the Loch Awe mountains, the great trench of Glen Kinglass cuts across the land from Loch Etive in the west to Victoria Bridge near Bridge of Orchy in the east. The glen separates the Loch Awe Munros from a group of five disparate Munros further north, known as the Glen Etive Group after their primary access point.

The Glen Etive road runs a gauntlet of mountains for 12ml/19km, threading its way southwards from the east entrance of Glen Coe to the head of Loch Etive. The five Munros of the Glen Etive Group stand on the east side of the road near its foot.

The foot of the glen is dominated by the massive bulk and airy twin summits of Ben Starav, the highest Munro of the group, but it is not an easy mountain to climb. Three of the other four Munros also require determination to reach, as ascent routes variously negotiate slopes that are steep and rocky and ridges that are narrow and exposed.

Meall nan Eun, the lowest of the quintet, is an exception and can be climbed without difficulty (unless the cloud descends, but when does that ever happen in Scotland?).

It has to be said that the peak is no great shakes to look at. Lying to the north of its neighbours, it is a heap of a thing with a flat, scraggy summit dome. From most angles, as in the above picture, it looks like a great pudding, with steep craggy sides that deter ascent. Only in the direction of Glen Etive to the west does it fortuitously permit an easy approach.

Viewed from the Glen Etive roadside, it loiters at the end of the long, broad-bottomed Glen Ceitlein (*Katelyn*), if you can distinguish it at all. Unexpectedly, however, the stroll up the glen constitutes the most pleasant approach walk in Glen Etive. And from its head a path will take you all the way to Eun's retiring summit.

Meall nan Eun from Coileitir (Glen Etive)
136468 NN 136468, 10ml/16km, 900m/2950ft

The route begins on the access track to the cottage at Coileitir, 2½ml/4km from Glen Etive road end (roadside parking). The track bridges the River Etive. One hundred metres beyond the bridge, branch left on another track to the foot of Glen Ceitlein, then branch right on yet another track that goes up the almost level glen on the north (left-hand) side of the river.

When the track ends, a path continues, crossing grassy flats and passing beautiful waterslides to reach an immense basin at the foot of several peaks.

The hillsides surrounding the basin glisten with rock slabs and tumbling streams, to such a confusing extent that it is difficult to determine precisely which summit is which on the undulating skyline. Meall nan Eun is the highpoint to the right of the flat bealach seen ahead, not to be confused (as it often is) with the heap of Meall Odhar (*Myowl Oa-ar*, Dun-coloured Hill) further left.

The solution to the confusion is simple: don't lose the continuing rough path beside the stream that comes down from the bealach right of Meall nan Eun (NN 183451).

The approach to the bealach

For most of the ascent the path stays on the left side of the stream, but higher up, nearing the bealach, the stream enters a small gorge and the path moves to the right.

Above the gorge, a small defile continues to the bealach itself, and from hereon the ascent of Meall nan Eun couldn't be simpler. Only 130m/400ft of gentle heath separate you from the wide open expanses of the gritty ▲summit dome.

The summit (yes, really!) of MEALL NAN EUN

▲Stob Ghabhar 55 1090m/3576ft (OS 50, NN 230455)
Stop Go-er, Goat Peak

Viewed from Stob a' Choire Odhair

E ast of Glen Etive, the four bold Munros of the Black Mount Range form an eye-catching quartet on the western edge of Rannoch Moor. The name comes from the Gaelic Am Monadh Dubh (*Doo*, Black), in contrast to Am Monadh Liath (*Lee-a*, Grey) further east.

As the A82 snakes its way north around the range from Bridge of Orchy to Glen Coe, every bend in the road reveals some new photogenic view of the mountains across a foreground of moor and lochan. But such is their topographical complexity that passing drivers are granted only a distant glimpse of their alluring interior.

And there's even better news... in addition to looking handsome from afar, the peaks are even more beguiling once you get among them. This guidebook describes routes up

three of the four Munros.

At the southern end of the range, multi-faceted Stob Ghabhar is one impressive mountain, so finely sculpted that it would not look out of place in the exalted confines of Glen Coe further up the A82. The 400m/1300ft cliffs of its yawning eastern corrie (Coirein Lochain, *Corry-in Lochin*, Corrie of the Lochan) rise directly to the summit.

The peak is often climbed along with its satellite Munro Stob a' Choire Odhair (Route 5), which stands guard at the corrie entrance, but the awkward connecting ridge (known as Aonach Eagach, *Ernach Aikach*, Notched Ridge) should be avoided by anyone who feels uncomfortable on unstable ground. You can reach Stob Ghabhar more easily by the route described here.

Stob Ghabhar from Victoria Bridge
NN 271418, 10ml/16km, 940m/3100ft

The route begins at Victoria Bridge car park, 400m from the end of the A8005 from Bridge of Orchy. Walk to the bridge and take the track that heads west along the Abhainn Shirra. After 1ml/1½km, at the foot of the evocatively named Allt Toaig (*Owlt Toe-ig*, Stream of the Fit of Passion), you'll reach Clashgour Hut, a small green building that was once a schoolhouse but which is now used by Glasgow University Mountaineering Club.

Your next goal is Clashgour farm, which lies a further 1½ml/2km away along the track. In dry weather it is more pleasant to take the slightly longer riverbank path to the Allt Ghabhar and then another track from there to the farm.

At the right-hand bend just before the farm buildings, bear left on an initially overgrown track beside a ruined wall. This is an old stalkers' path, now maintained as an ATV track in its lower section. It crosses the Allt Ghabhar (bridge), exits the forest and runs up Coire Ghabhar, Stob Ghabhar's deep southern corrie.

In the bowl of the corrie the path becomes rougher and indistinct as it climbs more steeply onto the corrie's grassy left-hand hillside. Despite being overgrown, it nevertheless continues to provide fair going as far as its end, above which 200m/650ft of grass separates you from the skyline.

STOB GHABHAR

Sron a' Ghearrain

Here you stand on the Bealach Coire Laoghan (*Leu-an*, Calves), named for the corrie on the other side of the ridge. Stob Ghabhar's two western Tops lie to each side.

Off-route to the west, but easily bagged (it's only 40m/130ft higher) is ΔStob a Bhruaich Leith (*Stop a*

Vroo-ich Lyay, Peak of the Grey Slope). To the east, a great swathe of grass climbs gently to the rounded top of ΔSron a' Ghearrain (*Strawn a Yarrin*, Nose of the Gelding). Then the grassy ridge narrows pleasantly across a small dip before rising to Stob Ghabhar's ▲summit.

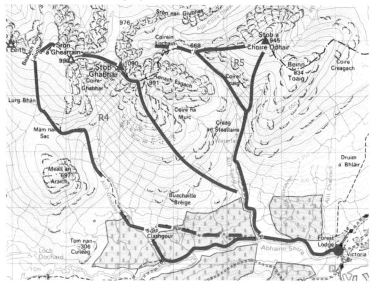

For a round trip, head south-west down to the cairned rise at the junction of the north and west rims of Coire na Muic (*Corra na Moo-ichk*, Corrie of the Pig). Avoid the narrow north rim (Aonach Eagach) by bearing right down the broad west rim on easy slopes of grass and rocks. This ridge separates Corrie na Muic from Coire Ghabhar.

The start of the descent of Coire na Muic's west rim

After a stroll to the far corner of the rim, stony ground is left behind for rough, steep grass slopes that descend all the way to the Allt Toaig. You can recce these on the outward journey. They will give no difficulty as long as you stay well right of rocky ground below the mouth of Coire na Muic, where An Steallaire (*An Shtyowllera*, The Cascade) tumbles down to the Allt Toaig. A good plan is to aim for the forest edge at NN 252432.

Prepare for a bracing splash across the Allt Toaig to reach a stalkers' path that will take you down to Clashgour Hut to rejoin the approach route.

STOB GHABHAR   Aonach Eagach

Coire na Muic

easy

scrambling route

An Steallaire ——

▲Stob a' Choire Odhair 226 945m/3100ft
(OS 50, NN 257459) *Stop a Chorra Oa-er*, Peak of the Dun Corrie

STOB A'
CHOIRE ODHAIR

STOB GHABHAR

Viewed from the A82

When viewed from the A82 across the watery wastes of Rannoch Moor, even mighty Stob Ghabhar is overshadowed by its neighbour Stob a' Choire Odhair. Its sweeping eastern slopes rise directly from moor to summit, half-blocking the higher peak from sight and giving some indication of what a good viewpoint it is.

It is difficult to avoid comparing the two contrasting Stobs, and there is no doubt that Ghabhar is the more distinguished peak. Beside it, Stob a' Choire Odhair does suffer an unfortunate tendency to lumpenness, but then so would most mountains.

Although it may lack craggy corries and rocky ridges, you'll nevertheless get to see plenty of scenery on what is a surprisingly straightforward ascent route. And on descent you can even visit Stob Ghabhar's hidden gem, the majestic Coirein Lochain itself.

Of all the mountains on the edge of Rannoch Moor, Stob a' Choire Odhair lays claim to being the best viewpoint. Not only does the summit provide immense views of the moor and its flanking Munros, but the view into the heart of Coirein Lochain, with its lochan and waterfalls backed by soaring cliffs, is as grand a mountainscape as you could wish for in the Central Highlands. Picture on Page 13.

Stob a' Choire Odhair from Victoria Bridge
NN 271418, 8ml/13km, 780m/2550ft

Park at Victoria Bridge car park, 400m from the end of the A8005 from Bridge of Orchy. Walk to the bridge and take the track that heads west along the Abhainn Shirra. After 1ml/1½km, at the foot of the Allt Toaig (*Owlt Toe-ig*, Stream of the Fit of Passion), you'll reach Clashgour Hut, a small green building that was once a schoolhouse but which is now used by Glasgow University Mountaineering Club. At the bridge just beyond, leave the track for a stalkers' path that climbs beside the Allt Toaig.

Although the path is wet in places and rough higher up, it nevertheless gives an excellent approach walk. On its left as you ascend is An Steallaire (*An Shtyowllera*, The Cascade), a multi-tiered waterfall that drops from Stob Ghabhar's south-eastern corrie

An Steallaire is passed on the Allt Toaig path

(Coire na Muic, *Moo-ichk*, Pig). Ahead, the ascent route up Stob a' Choire Odhair's grassy south-west spur is seen in its entirety. Ironically, the path's directness and gentleness encourage a rate of knots that renders the approach a more tiring promenade than it seems it should be.

Stay on the stalkers' path as far as the stream that comes down from the bealach (NN 253446) between Stob a' Choire Odhair and Beinn Toaig. N.B. The path continues beyond here to the foot of a series of small waterfalls on the Allt Taoig. Beyond these, a rougher boot-worn path continues up a shallow upper corrie (Coire

W Ridge   STOB A' CHOIRE ODHAIR
SW Spur
Allt Taoig

The map for this route is combined with that for Stob Ghabhar on Page 15.

Taoig) to the bealach at its head, between Stob Ghabhar and Stob a' Choire Odhair. This route will be used for the return journey.

For now, leave the path c.20m past the stream, which can be a nuisance to cross when in spate. A steeper, drier baggers' path climbs straight up the south-west spur, which forms the left-hand side of the stream. The path takes a steep, direct line at first but relents higher up when the Stob generously deigns to provide a welcome set of zigzags. Above these, gentler slopes of grass and rocks, among which the path becomes indistinct, lead to the ▲summit.

Continuing in the direction of Stob Ghabhar, a stony path runs down Stob a' Choire Odhair's gentle west ridge to the intervening bealach, where it joins the upper end of the Allt Taoig path noted above.

Before descending, it is worth a detour to the lochan at the heart of Coirein Lochain, hidden to the right around the foot of a rocky spur. The encircling cliffs will make you feel very small indeed.

▲Meall a' Bhuiridh 45 1108m/3635ft (OS 41, NN 251503)
Myowl a Voory, Hill of Rutting or Roaring (of deer)

MEALL A' BHUIRIDH

Viewed from the A82

Further up the A82 from Stob a' Choire Odhair (Route 5), Meall a' Bhuiridh is yet another prominent Black Mount Munro revealed to advantage across the watery wastes of Rannoch Moor. Like Stob a' Choire Odhair it can't compete with Stob Ghabhar (Route 4) for mountain form, but it can certainly challenge the range's most celebrated peak for interest of ascent.

A glance at the map will tell you something else. At its north end the Black Mount comes to an abrupt halt at Meall a' Bhuiridh, and its situation at the junction of Glen Coe and Rannoch Moor affords views to make showier peaks green with envy.

The standard ascent route begins at Glencoe Mountain Resort and climbs through Coire Pollach (Peaty Corrie). Such are the snow-holding properties of this open, north-facing corrie that it became Scotland's first mechanised downhill ski centre, yet on foot in summer the route through it is without difficulty.

A continuation to neighbouring Creise (*Kraysha*, origin dubious), the Black Mount's fourth Munro, is a more difficult proposition as it requires handwork on a rocky spur.

At the time of writing, the car park café and ski slopes access chairlift at Glencoe Mountain Resort are open throughout the summer from 9.00 (8.00 at weekends) to 16.30. By using the chairlift you can reach a height of 670m/2200ft in Coire Pollach in a seated position. What do you mean, it's cheating? Don't you use a car to get to the car park at 360m/1200ft?

The Eagle's Rest Café in Coire Pollach may also be open in high summer. For more info. see www.glencoemountain.com, phone 01855-851-226 or enquire at Glencoe Visitor Centre, where there's also a café and shop (NN 112575, www.glencoe-nts.org.uk, tel: 0844-493-2222).

Meall a' Bhuiridh from Glencoe Mountain Resort
NN 266525, 4ml/7km, 750m/2450ft

From Glencoe Mountain Resort car park, just off the A82 near the Glen Etive turn-off, your first objective is Coire Pollach. Only you know whether you deem it conscionable to use the chairlift. The path begins at the very road end, on the right opposite the last building. The steep, stony ascent beneath the chairlift is a rough way to start the day.

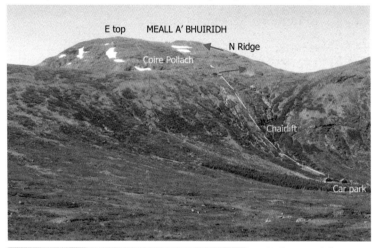

E top   MEALL A' BHUIRIDH   N Ridge
Coire Pollach
Chairlift
Car park

Coire Pollach

Looking down the north ridge

At the top of the chairlift, follow the dirt road across the corrie to its end at the building known as the Plateau Café (closed in summer). The easiest route up from here avoids the steepest slopes directly ahead by bearing right onto the north ridge, where the angle eases.

As height is gained, grass gives way to rock rubble up which, if you're lucky, you'll find a stony path to ease the final ascent to the ▲summit.

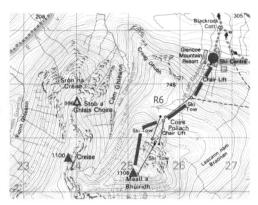

Over the summit, a path makes a short descent across boulders to a minor dip, where a T-bar tow tops out. From here, a short bouldery ridge runs out to the lower east top, which is worth the short detour for the uninterrupted views it affords over Rannoch Moor.

MEALL A' BHUIRIDH

E top

To take advantage of any snow still lying around in upper Coire Pollach, it is tempting to bound down beside the ski tows, but steep, craggy ground lies hidden out of sight below in the vicinity of the Cliffhanger Chairlift. Unless you are prepared to navigate a way down steep, rocky terrain, avoid temptation.

Mutual surprise   MEALL A' BHUIRIDH

Viewed from Creise summit plateau

In 1956 the north-facing bowl of Coire Pollach became home to the first Scottish ski tow. In the following year Bill Smith used the new tow to ski the first 'Everest' in Scotland – 34,000ft (10,370m) of downhill in one day.

▲Beinn Fhionnlaidh 149 959m/3146ft (OS 50, NN 095497)
Ben *Hyoonly*, Finlay's Mountain

Viewed from the east across Glen Etive

BEINN FHIONNLAIDH   Pt 841

The district of Appin lies between Glen Etive and the west coast. In the south, Loch Creran and Glen Creran cut deep into its heart to form a peninsula to the west. The name Appin strictly applies only to this peninsula, which contains two Munros in the Beinn a' Bheithir massif (Route 8), but the district boundaries are commonly extended to include three more Munros that line up on the east side of Glen Creran.

Of the three, Beinn Sgulaird and Sgor na h-Ulaidh are complex mountains that sport adventurous ascent routes, but Beinn Fhionnlaidh has a much simpler profile and is easier to climb.

Tucked away at the head of Glen Creran, sandwiched between Beinn Sgulaird and Sgor na h-Ulaidh, hidden in the interior between Glen Creran and Glen Etive and surrounded by forests on three sides, it is perhaps the least known of all the Munros of the Central Highlands.

In shape it consists almost entirely of a single ridge, some 4m/7km long, which rises gradually from the west to cross the summit and end abruptly at a minor east top (Point 841 on OS map). East of the summit the ridge is rocky and narrow, but an approach via the west ridge from Glen Creran avoids all difficulty and has the advantage of great west coast views.

Beinn Fhionnlaidh from Elleric (Glen Creran)
NN 035488, 9ml/14km, 960m/3150ft

Unlike Beinn Fhionnlaidh's sharp east ridge, its west ridge rises without incident all the way from glen to summit. Features of interest along the way are few and far between, and this makes for either a prolonged plod or a carefree jaunt, according to inclination. Whatever you view of the ascent, you can be assured of a free-wheelin' ride back down.

BEINN FHIONNLAIDH

Viewed from the west from Glen Creran

Begin at the car park at the end of the public road near Elleric in Glen Creran. Take the private road to Glenure House then the Land Rover track that goes left into upper Glen Creran. A couple of hundred metres beyond Glenure House, the track crosses a stream (bridge). Less than 100m further along, a rough track on the right climbs through woods onto open hillside.

From the end of the track a path continues up the little grassy ridge ahead, passing a tree growing out of a boulder. It improves with height and eventually contours across Fhionnlaidh's southern flanks.

BEINN FHIONNLAIDH

Lochan Cairn Deirg

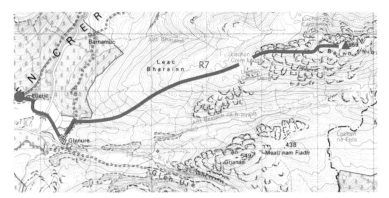

To gain the west ridge, leave the path after a mile or so to climb the sprawling grassy hillside above, oddly named the Leac Bharrain (*Lyechk Varrin*, Thorny Slab).

Over the skyline, almost two-thirds of the way up in height but only half-way in distance (patience, patience), is a levelling that boasts the route's only features of interest: a couple of lochans and some large erratic boulders. The larger lochan glories under the name of Lochan Cairn Deirg (*Lochan Cairn Jerrik*, Lochan of the Red Cairn).

Above here the terrain becomes more rugged and boulder-strewn, but the going improves and there's now an intermittent path. The ridge begins to take more shape as it rims Fhionnlaidh's north face, which sports sizeable swathes of good clean rock.

Viewed from the north from Sgor na h-Ulaidh

BEINN FHIONNLAIDH

West Spur

North Face

If you want a break from the ascent make a short detour left onto the craggy west spur of the face, to view the summit above the slabs. The ▲summit lies not far beyond.

On descent, once you've reached the lower slopes, beyond all crags, remember to aim left to rejoin the approach path and find better going. All the way down, as reward for your endeavours, you'll have gravity going for you and a panoramic view of the western seaboard, hopefully glistening beneath a westering sun.

Point 841, at the foot of the upper east ridge, is noteworthy both for its unsurpassed views of the Glen Etive mountains and for its summit quartzite, which is among the purest white to be found on any Scottish mountain. However, to reach it you'd have to scramble down a couple of rock steps on the ridge crest, or take an exposed bypass path.

BEINN FHIONNLAIDH

rock steps

E Ridge

Viewed from Pt 841

Thanks to its temperate west coast climate, Appin and its surrounding area boast numerous gardens to visit on an off-day.

Pick up leaflets at Ballachulish Visitor Centre or Glencoe Visitor Centre, or visit the website: www.gardens-of-argyll.co.uk.

▲Sgorr Dhearg 107 1024m/3360ft (OS 41, NN 056558)
Skorr Jerrak, Red Peak

BEINN A' BHEITHIR

Sgorr Bhan — SGORR DHEARG — SGORR DHONUILL — SW Ridge — Gleann a' Chaolais — Loch Linnhe

At the north end of Appin the beautifully proportioned massif of Beinn a' Bheithir (*Ben a Vay-hir*, Mountain of the Serpent) towers over the narrows that separate Loch Linnhe from Loch Leven west of Glencoe. Its three highpoints are a familiar sight to drivers crossing the Ballachulish Bridge, which spans the narrows.

The centre peak (Sgorr Dhearg) and western peak (Sgorr Dhonuill, *Skorr Ghaw-il*, Donald's Peak) are both Munros, while the eastern peak (Sgorr Bhan, *Skorr Vahn*, White Peak) is a Top. The ridge linking the two Munros gives a classic ridge walk, especially when approached by a scramble up the soaring north-east ridge of Sgorr Bhan, but this is no route for anyone who prefers to rule adrenaline surges out of their life.

The section of ridge between the two Munros forms the rim of the great northern corrie of Gleann a' Chaolais (anglicised to Glenachulish, *Glen-a-Hoolish*, Glen of the Narrows). On the map, if Sgorr Bhan is to be excluded, the obvious line of attack is a horseshoe round of the skyline, going up one Munro and down the other. However, even this is not easy, courtesy of Sgorr Dhonuill's abrupt summit. Moreover, blanket afforestation dictates alternative approaches, using recently constructed paths through the trees.

The current standard ascent route climbs to the bealach between the two Munros. Once there, Sgorr Dhearg is easily climbed by its south-west ridge, described here. On the other side of the bealach, Sgorr Dhonuill's east ridge rears up more challengingly, with a rocky, scrambly, exposed upper section that is no place for those of a sensitive disposition.

While in the area, don't miss impressive Inchree Falls just north of Onich across Loch Leven (NN 031629). The upper steps in a staircase of eight falls, including a 15m/50ft drop, can be seen from a viewpoint reached by a woodland walk.

Sgorr Dhearg from Glenachulish
NN 047589, 7ml/11km, 980m/3200ft

Begin at Glenachulish car park, reached by a short paved road from the A828 just west of Ballachulish Bridge. Your first objective is the upper forest boundary. Follow the route described here carefully to find your way through the labyrinth of forest roads, even when it appears to be taking you in the wrong direction.

SGORR DHEARG

N Ridge

SW Ridge

From the car park, take the forest road up Gleann a' Chaolais on the west (right-hand) side of the river. The bealach ahead, left of Sgorr a' Chaolais, is the one you're aiming for. At a fork after several hundred metres (NN 047582), branch left across the river (bridge) then immediately right on a grassier track that climbs through the forest and doubles back to reach a higher forest road.

Go straight across this road to find a continuing path-cum-track that, like the previous one, climbs right before doubling back left to reach a still higher forest road, just before the vehicle turning circle at its end (NN 049573). Go straight across the road

again to find a recently constructed path to the bealach, which begins as an obvious staircase of large rocks.

This new path consigns to history the old path, which begins beside a concrete bridge a few hundred metres back down the road. The old path is exasperatingly steep, worn and muddy but is still used by those who have not had the foresight to purchase a superior guidebook.

The new path makes a short climb left before turning right to make a rising traverse across the hillside in the direction of the bealach, which can now be seen directly ahead. At times

The name *Beithir* (aspirated to *Bheithir*) is variously translated as serpent, demon or thunderbolt, and all three are correct! Beithir was a Celtic goddess with a dual personality. Youthful and beautiful on a good hair day, when crossed she could

become a fickle, serpentine demon raining thunderbolts. She was reputed to live locally on her eponymous mountain and was blamed for all manner of natural disasters (storms, floods etc.). Tread carefully lest you incur her wrath.

Sgorr a' Chaolais

Bealach

The new path through the forest

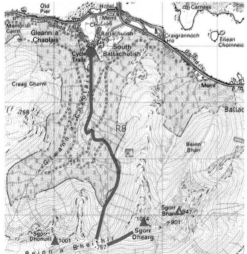

the path crosses open hillside, at other times it burrows through dark forest with a fairytale ambience.

Eventually the path rounds the top of the trees, crosses a fence and reaches a second fence, where the less distinct old path comes up from the right and the new path ends (NN 050564). Immediately beyond the path junction, the going deteriorates on a short traverse across the hillside into the corrie below the bealach.

Above right as you climb through the forest you'll get glimpses of the rock pyramid of Sgorr a' Chaolais, also known as The Dragon's Tooth (unnamed on OS map). This forms the end point of a short, sharp little ridge that juts northwards over Gleann a' Chaolais from near the summit of Sgorr Dhonuill. It is an unsurprisingly little-trodden summit that offers no way up for walkers.

The corrie flats are quite a comedown after the excellent going so far. Marshy enough to test patience as well as the waterproofness of boots, the wet ground necessitates numerous detours and much leaping. At the head of the corrie, still following the fence, the path climbs rougher, steeper and still boggy slopes to gain the bealach.

Exiting the trees

Bealach

The going now improves again on Sgorr Dhearg's broad south-west ridge, which climbs 270m/900ft from bealach to summit. The initial turf slopes are a joy to tread, and the zigzagging path makes short work of the stony upper slopes of pink quartzite that give the mountain its name. Soon you'll be standing at the viewsome pyramid ▲summit.

SGORR DHEARG

BIDEAN NAM BIAN

Bealach

SGORR DHONUILL

SGORR DHEARG

East of Sgorr Dhearg's summit the narrow rim of Coire Giubhsachain (*Corra Gewsachin*, Corrie of the Pines) curves to ΔSgorr Bhan, forming a beautiful symmetrical arc. A path runs all the way along the quartzite rubble crest.

The ridge is quite narrow in places, with steep drops on each side, but the uniform angle and lack of any great exposure ensure that its negotiation is never more than a walk. Any takers? (return trip: 1ml/1½km, 170m/550ft).

SGORR DHONUILL

Bealach

Viewed from Sgorr Dhearg

The 240m/800ft climb from the bealach to the summit of Sgorr Dhonuill begins on grass slopes steep enough for the path to have eroded into a stony rut. The angle eases to a levelling then steeper slopes rise to a second levelling. Finally the ridge narrows and steepens even more to the rocky summit pyramid, with considerable exposure on the scrambly rim of a craggy corrie.

Buachaille Etive Beag:
Boo-achilya Etive Bake, Little Herdsman of Etive
▲**Stob Dubh** 201 958m/3143ft (OS 41, NN 179535)
Stop Doo, Black Peak
▲**Stob Coire Raineach** 263 925m/3035ft (OS 41,
NN 191548) *Stop Corra Raynach*, Peak of the Corrie of Bracken

BUACHAILLE ETIVE BEAG

STOB COIRE RAINEACH

Stob nan Cabar

STOB DUBH   Pt 902

Lairig Gartain

At its eastern head, 310m/1000ft above the village at its foot, Glen Coe opens out onto the wide spaces of Rannoch Moor, where the horizontal meets the vertical at two great mountains: Buachaille Etive Mor (*Moar*, Big) and Buachaille Etive Beag.

They face each other across the Lairig Gartain (*Lahrik Garstin*, Pass of the Ticks) and are uncannily similar in shape, each bearing two Munros. The spectacular arrowhead of the *Big Buchel* (as it is known to legions of hillwalkers) is Scotland's premier rock climbing draw and is a challenging mountain to climb. The *Wee Buchel*, though not much smaller, is more accommodating to those of us who are allergic to rock.

Like its big sibling, it presents an intimidatingly rocky north end to Glen Coe (Stob nan Cabar, *Stop nan Cabbar*, Antler Peak). Beyond here a fine ridge is slung between the two Munros. The 748m/2455ft bealach between the two allows access either from the Lairig Gartain to the east or from the Lairig Eilde (*Lahrik Ailtya*, Pass of the Hinds) to the west.

The slopes on each side of the bealach are quite steep but on the Lairig Eilde side there is a renovated path all the way up. From the bealach, you can bag each Munro in turn.

Stob Dubh from Glen Coe
NN 188563, 4ml/7km, 710m/2350ft

The route begins at the Glen Coe end of the Lairig Eilde. The Allt Lairig Eilde drops into the glen at a popular roadside waterfall and the path begins at a car park a few hundred metres east along the road.

STOB COIRE RAINEACH

Pt 902

Bealach

STOB DUBH

Lairig Eilde

A82

Recently renovated, the stony-surfaced ribbon of a path starts on the left-hand (east) side of the stream before crossing to the right-hand (west) side to negotiate the upper

reaches of the pass. Leave it at a cairned fork after only c.600m, just before it bears right across the hillside to the stream crossing, to branch left on the earthier Buachaille Etive Beag path. Yes, you're right, that earthiness implies bogginess after rain.

The further of the two pointed peaks seen ahead on the left-hand skyline is Stob Dubh, while the nearer peak to its left is not Stob Coire Raineach but Point 902, a minor top on the ridge to Stob Dubh. You are aiming to reach the skyline at the bealach on the near side of Point 902.

The path climbs diagonally across the hillside to a small streamlet, then heads straight for the skyline up an almost continuous man-made rock staircase. It is tough on the knees but height is gained fast, and it is always worth a stop to admire the view back across Glen Coe to Aonach Eagach.

When the steps end, the angle eases and the path crosses several streamlets that descend this part of the hillside. This section can be boggy in places, but at the time of writing the NTS is restoring the path. The bealach rewards with an attention-grabbing view across the Lairig Gartain to the multi-topped skyline of Buachaille Etive Mor.

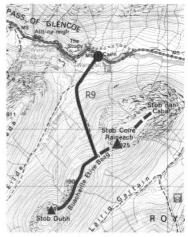

Steep slopes of rock-strewn grass rise on each side of the bealach, carrying rough, stony paths to each Munro. The climb to Stob Dubh begins steeply but, after reaching Point 902, the character of the route improves dramatically. A curving ridge, becoming narrower and rockier as it progresses, gives superb ridge walking on a gently undulating descent to a dip beneath Stob Dubh. The stony path then heads skywards once more to surmount a final steepening and gain Stob Dubh's pyramid ▲summit.

The superb view south along Glen Etive leads the eye between flanking mountains to Loch Etive. For the full effect, wander beyond the summit, across a couple of minor dips, to a cairned viewpoint.

Springtime on Buachaille Etive Beag

STOB DEARG

BUACHAILLE ETIVE MOR

Lairig Gartain

STOB DUBH

Bonus Munro: Stob Coire Raineach
add-on ¾ml/1km, 170m/550ft

After returning to the bealach from Stob Dubh, the climb up the other side to Stob Coire Raineach is steep but straightforward, enabling you to bag a tempting bonus Munro. The Wee Buachaille's subsidiary Stob only became a Munro in 1997 and the grittier, looser path to its summit reflects its shorter history in the Tables. Nevertheless, the path soon puts you at the scenic summit.

STOB COIRE RAINEACH

Bealach

Viewed from Pt 902

Stob Coire Raineach is a peerless viewpoint above Glen Coe. For the full effect, stroll out along the broad north-east ridge, past a couple of ridge-top lochans, to its end point at Stob nan Cabar for an 'eagle's eyrie' view of Aonach Eagach.

AONACH EAGACH

Glen Coe

The view from Stob nan Cabar

▲Bidean nam Bian 23 1150m/3773ft (OS 41, NN 143542)
Beejan nam Byann, Peak of the Mountains

Stob Coire nan Lochan — BIDEAN NAM BIAN — Stob Coire nam Beith
Third Sister — Coire nam Beith — Loch Achtriochtan

Viewed from Aonach Eagach

G len Coe, the most dramatic glen in the country, is squeezed between challenging Munros. The south side of the glen is dominated by the craggy buttresses of the Three Sisters, which support the tapering summit of Bidean nam Bian. The north side is dominated by the craggy wall of Aonach Eagach, whose pinnacled crest gives an exciting scramble.

Bidean, the highest peak not only in Glen Coe but in the whole of Argyll, is the supreme hillwalkers' mountain. Its airy summit forms the hub of more than 12ml/20km of high ridges that extend on all sides, most famously towards the glen, where three rocky spurs terminate abruptly above the road to form the Three Sisters.

The numerous interlocking ridges

and corries produce a topography so intricate that you can climb Bidean from different sides and find it hard to believe that it's the same mountain.

The standard approach route, which also gives access to the satellite Munro of Stob Coire Sgreamhach (*Stop Corra Screvach*, Peak of the Horrible Corrie), climbs the Lost Valley between the first and second Sisters, but the steep, loose exit to the skyline is no place for sensitive souls.

For an easy way up there's a choice of one: via Coire nam Beith (*Corra nam Bay*, Corrie of the Birches) west of the Three Sisters. Despite its lack of technical difficulty it is no bridesmaid route as it passes through some of the most imposing rock scenery on the mountain.

Bidean nam Bian from Loch Achtriochtan (Glen Coe)
NN 138566, 5ml/8km, 1100m/36000ft

Of the three ridges that meet at Bidean's summit, the one that curves north-west around the rim of Coire nam Beith is the easiest. The route up the corrie was once a popular approach but, since the elevation of Stob Coire Sgreamhach to Munro status in 1997, the shortest ascent route to both peaks has moved further east to the Lost Valley.

The Coire nam Beith route still provides the shortest route from the roadside to Bidean's summit, takes you to the heart of Bidean's most impressive rockscapes and carries the only renovated path on the mountain that goes all the way to the skyline.

Begin at a gate on the west side of the road bridge over the River Coe at the west end of Loch Achtriochtan (car

park on east side). The path initially climbs the steep hillside ahead, right of a prominent waterfall, and is a rock staircase for much of the way.

The only obstacle is a short, slabby section of rock hidden in a band of trees below the waterfall. Its negotiation requires a spot of hand-work that may give brief pause for thought, but it is such a minor obstacle in a benign situation low down on the mountain that we are confident you can conquer it. Above here the 'staircase' climbs beside the waterfall in a series of tight zigzags, with increasingly panoramic views back across Glen Coe to Aonach Eagach. How many zigzags? Best not to ask.

Above the waterfall, beneath the craggy west face of Aonach Dubh (*Ernach Doo*, Black Ridge – the Third Sister), the path enters a ravine, temporarily loses the battle with

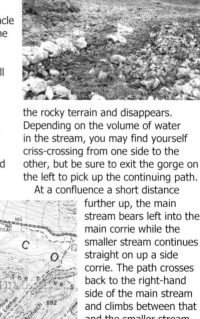

Glen Coe   Looking back down the route to the Bealach an t-Sron

the rocky terrain and disappears. Depending on the volume of water in the stream, you may find yourself criss-crossing from one side to the other, but be sure to exit the gorge on the left to pick up the continuing path.

At a confluence a short distance

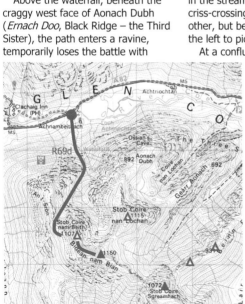

further up, the main stream bears left into the main corrie while the smaller stream continues straight on up a side corrie. The path crosses back to the right-hand side of the main stream and climbs between that and the smaller stream, beside an even smaller streamlet, to the foot of cliffs, where you reach a path junction at the top of a long flight of stone steps.

The route onwards takes the right branch, but a brief note on the left branch is in order as it continues up the main corrie. Unfortunately it leads to nowhere useful unless you wish to view or climb some rock. It climbs beside waterfalls into Bidean nam Bian's craggy heartland, with Diamond Buttress and Church Door Buttress looming ahead beneath the summit.

Bealach an t-Sron

Leaving the main corrie to rock climbers, take the right fork at the path junction – a renovated path that climbs a side corrie to the Bealach an t-Sron (NN 134547, named only on OS 1:25,000 map), between An t-Sron (*An Drawn*, The Shoulder) and Stob Coire nam Beith. The path climbs the left side of the small stream noted above and, for a while, is quite rough in places. As you look up to the skyline, a scree slope high on the left appears to offer the easiest way up, but stick to the streamside path as it climbs into a small basin hidden further right.

Above here, there is no sign of the path up the horrendous boulderfield that rises in front of you to the skyline, but fear not – it is hidden among the boulders. It's rough and it's stony but, with well-contoured zigzags, it makes surprisingly light work of the ascent.

You emerge onto the skyline at the bealach between An t-Sron and Stob Coire nam Beith, with glorious west coast views. A loose stony path continues up Bidean's north-west ridge along the cliff edge, climbing vast swathes of scree to the Δsummit of Stob Coire nam Beith.

Beyond here, the path crosses a dip to a stony minor top, then it crosses another dip before narrowing to Bidean's ▲summit. All the way up, there are dizzying cliff-edge views above Coire nam Beith, increasing in grandeur as well-named Diamond Buttress and Church Door Buttress

Bealach an t-Sron

BIDEAN NAM BIAN

come into view below the summit.

On descent, if you haven't taken careful note of the route on the way up (we don't mean *you*, of course), there are a couple of spots that may lead astray. To find the top of the path on the bealach between Stob Coire nam Beith and An t-Sron, pass a steep false start (blocked off by a wall of rocks) and do not descend until you reach a cairn from where the obvious path starts gently downhill.

Lower down, when the path becomes temporarily lost in the ravine above the lower waterfall, it can be hard to find the restart. Exit the ravine on the left and you'll find branch paths that will take you to it.

From the Glen Coe roadside it is difficult to get a view of Bidean's retiring summit behind the Three Sisters. The best vantage point is the flat-topped rock outcrop known as The Study (NN 183564). Stroll out to it along the old Glen Coe road, which can be gained without a river crossing at NN 194564 (parking nearby).

The Three Sisters of Glen Coe

The old road to The Study.

▲Mullach nan Coirean 236 939m/3081ft
(OS 41, NN 122662) *Mullach nan Corran*, Summit of the Corries

The Mamores are a range of ten Munros and seven Tops that form a mountainous palisade north of Glen Coe, between Loch Leven and Glen Nevis. They are characterised by the attractive conical peaks that give the range its evocative if brazen name, meaning Big Breasts. Add to that a narrow skyline reached by a selection of excellent stalkers' paths and you have a range that was designed for ridge-walking. This guidebook features routes up five of the Munros.

No two neighbouring peaks could contrast more starkly than the two most westerly Mamores: Mullach nan Coirean and Stob Ban (*Stop Bahn*, White Peak). The Stob is a great white cone of quartzite, while the Mullach is a flat granite summit given shape by radiating ridges. In practice their differing characteristics complement each other so well that a trip to the Mullach's summit acts as a unique crash course in varieties of mountain form and colour.

Stob Ban is a more awkward peak to reach but you'll get stunning views of it from the Mullach. The normal route climbs the Mullach's easy north-east ridge on the rim of Coire Dearg (*Corra Jerrak*, Red Corrie), the largest and most interesting of all the corries that give the mountain its name.

Cameras at the ready. As the most westerly Munro, Mullach nan Coirean offers stunning aerial views of the Western Highlands across Loch Linnhe, with Munro upon Munro laid out for your viewing pleasure.

To the left the Nevis Range and the Grey Corries fill the sky. To the right are the Munros of Glen Coe and Appin. Ahead, the spine of the Mamores stretches away into the distance, bristling with summits.

Adding to the picturesqueness of the scene is a unique colour palette, with the red granite of the Mullach giving way to the white quartzite of Stob Ban. Brilliant!

Mullach nan Coirean from Glen Nevis
NN 145683, 5ml/8km, 890m/2900ft

The route begins at the car park in Glen Nevis, just before the road crosses the Water of Nevis at Polldubh Falls. Walk a couple of hundred metres back along the road and start up a forest track that climbs into Coire Dearg. You can avoid the first long switchback by taking a shortcut path signposted 'Forest Walk',

which forks left c.50m from the road.

The path climbs past a waterfall and rejoins the track higher up. Turn left here to follow the track around an immediate right-hand bend and across the forested lower slopes of Mullach nan Coirean's north-east ridge. Ignore a side track on the left half-way along

and, after c.800m, just before the track bends left into the corrie beyond Coire Dearg, leave it for a forest path waymarked by a cairn and wooden steps. Rooty but reasonably dry, the path climbs through the trees to reach open ground at a stile over the upper forest fence (NN 133681).

The fence climbs left up the hillside onto the Mullach's north-east ridge and the path follows it, boggy at first but becoming rougher and drier as the angle steepens on approach to the crest.

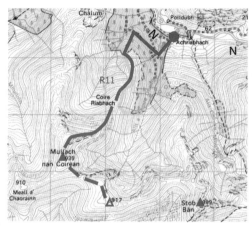

Once on the crest, the route improves immensely. The ridge is grassy and gentle, the path is good and views begin to build. At your back, the great lump of Ben Nevis towers over its glen, while across Coire Dearg to the left the white quartzite summits of Sgurr a' Mhaim and Stob Ban (often mistaken for snowcaps) become increasingly imposing. Note also the impressive rock tower on Stob Ban's north ridge, which must be crossed by scramblers contemplating a round of Coire Dearg's skyline.

When the fence ends, the ridge swings right, becoming steeper and more bouldery, but the good going continues all the way to the cairn at its top, at the junction with the broader north ridge. From here a short stroll across a bouldery plateau takes you around Coire Dearg's craggy rim to the Mullach's ▲summit.

SGURR A' MHAIM

Glen Nevis

Looking down the NE Ridge

South-west of Mullach nan Coirean's summit, a beautifully proportioned grassy ridge curves around the rim of Coire a' Mhuilinn (*Voolin*, Mill) to Meall a' Chaorainn for an uninterrupted view over Loch Linnhe. Well worth a look.

MEALL A' CHAORAINN

Coire a' Mhuilinn

MULLACH NAN COIREAN

Bonus Top: SE Top add-on return 1½ml/2½km, 160m/500ft

For a taster of Mamores ridge walking, why not take a stroll out along Coire Dearg's rim to the Mullach's SE Top before descending? The complete 2ml/3km walk to Stob Ban is one of the most scenic high-level walks in the Highlands and this first section is a joy to walk.

A gritty path runs close to the cliff edge on lawn-like terrain, swinging left, then right, then left again to the ΔSouth-east Top. You'll be loath to turn around and come back but, beyond the Top, the ridge becomes narrower and rockier, with no easy way off. An initial shallow dip separates you from a sharp-looking section of ridge that climbs a hump of red rock and you'll probably need no incentive to go no further.

STOB BAN

SE Top

MULLACH NAN COIREAN

▲Am Bodach 99 1032m/3386ft (OS 41, NN 176650)
Am Bottach, The Old Man

Am Bodach from the north

AM BODACH

STOB COIRE A' CHAIRN ←   NE Ridge   W Ridge

Coire a' Mhail

SGURR A' MHAIM

Am Bodach is a good-looking, pyramid-shaped peak that stands at the apex of three ridges. In some ways it is the most shapely of all the Mamores but, because its faces lack solid rock and its ridges lack exciting scrambling, it finds itself lower down the *Most Magnificent Mamore* pecking order than its appearance would otherwise merit.

The north-east ridge is steep and rubbly but the west ridge gives easy access to the summit from the south, especially as a stalkers' path climbs to its foot from Loch Leven. The remaining south-east ridge runs out to the outlying top of Sgorr an Fhuarain (*Skorr an Oo-arin*, Peak of the Spring), from where steeper, craggier slopes drop to Loch Leven.

The key to any ascent in the Mamores from the Loch Leven side is a Land Rover track that runs across the southern slopes of the range, reaching a low point of 200m/650ft at Mamore Lodge.

The track can be reached here by an access road that leaves the B863 just outside Kinlochleven at NN 175623. Refreshments are available at the lodge and you can park all day for a small fee. Should you feel it ethically reprehensible to ascend the first 200m/650ft by car, you'll find a network of paths that climb to the track from Kinlochleven.

Am Bodach from Mamore Lodge (Kinlochleven)
NN 186630, 7ml/11km, 830m/2700ft

On the Loch Leven side of Am Bodach a stalkers' path climbs to a height of over 750m/2450ft in the south-west corrie (Coire na h-Eirghe, poss. Coire na Eirighe, *Corra na Airee*, Corrie of Rising or Rebellion, unnamed on OS 1:50,000 map).

After parking at Mamore Lodge, go west along the Land Rover track for c.1½ml/2km, to the stream that drains the corrie. The stalkers' path begins on the high point of the next corner,

marked by a cairn on a trackside outcrop, c.100m beyond the bridge over the stream.

Follow the path up the corrie, first on the left side of the stream, then on the right. When it ends, a less well-engineered but still serviceable path continues up 120m/400ft of easy-angled grass and boulder slopes to the bealach between Sgorr an Iubhair (Skorr an Yoo-ir, Peak of the Yew, an easily baggable Top) and Am Bodach. Above here, with increasingly extensive Mamore views, the equally easy slopes of Am Bodach's west ridge rise pleasantly for a further 160m/500ft to the ▲summit.

On the map, a descent south-east from the summit to Sgorr an Fhuarain seems to open up the possibility of a round trip, but craggy slopes below complicate a descent either to Mamore Lodge or into lower Corra na Eirighe. Avoid.

From the foot of the west ridge a bypass path contours across Am Bodach's NW slopes to the foot of its NE ridge, from where Stob Coire a' Chairn can easily be climbed (see picture on Page 49).

NA GRUAGAICHEAN

AM BODACH

NE Ridge

W Ridge

Bypass path

Viewed from Sgorr an Iubhair

Am Bodach from the south

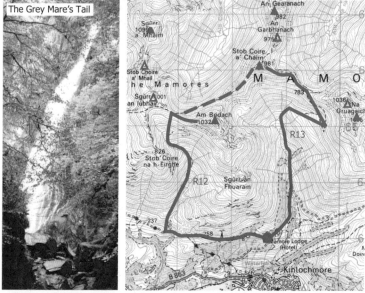

The Grey Mare's Tail

The Grey Mare's Tail is a beautiful 46m/ 175ft cascade near Kinlocheven. The trip to view it makes a good short walk if the tops are in cloud (or even if they're not). In low water you can reach the foot of the fall by a short boulder hop or paddle up the gorge below it, but take care on the mossy rocks.

The Grey Mare's Tail car park is beside St. Paul's Church, just off the B863 in the village (signposted).

▲Stob Coire a' Chairn 171 981m/3218ft (OS 41, NN 185660) *Stop Corra a Chairn*, Peak of the Corrie of the Cairn

Viewed from Am Bodach

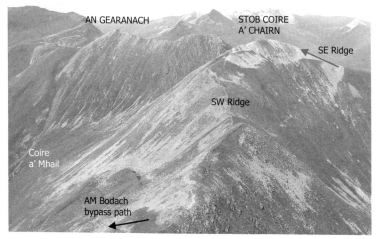

Like its neighbour Am Bodach, Stob Coire a' Chairn stands at the apex of three ridges. Unfortunately the resemblance ends there. It would appear that, once upon a time, the Stob was stamped on from a great height by a giant boot-heel, leaving a squashed summit atop featureless slopes. On the plus side, that makes it easier to climb than most Mamores and its central position in the range gives it excellent views of its fellows.

The south-west ridge climbs easily from the bealach at the foot of Am Bodach's north-east ridge, but the latter's steepness precludes a simple traverse from one Munro to the other. To avoid scrambling it would be necessary to use the stalkers' bypass path across Am Bodach's north-west slopes to connect with its easy west ridge (picture on Page 47).

The Stob's north-west ridge drops more steeply to the bealach below An Gearanach. It would be a feasible approach route except that there is no easy way to reach the bealach in the first place.

Fortunately the south-east ridge does offer an easy approach, courtesy of an excellent stalkers' path on the Stob's Loch Leven side. This climbs all the way to the foot of the ridge via the great southern corrie of Coire na Ba (*Corra na Bah*, Corrie of the Cattle, unnamed on OS 1:50,000 map).

Stob Coire a' Chairn from Mamore Lodge (Kinlochleven)
NN 186630, 7ml/11km, 680m/2250ft

From Mamore Lodge (see Page 46 for access), take the Land Rover track eastwards to the bridge over the Allt Coire na Ba, then the wide, initially stony, stalkers' path that heads up the corrie on the right side of the river.

AM BODACH

STOB COIRE
A' CHAIRN

Mamore
Lodge

Coire
na Ba

The path becomes indistinct in the boggy bowl of the corrie but improves again as it climbs out. It takes a long loop to the east to ease the angle of ascent on the steep corrie headwall and tops out on the bealach between Stob Coire a' Chairn and twin-topped Na Gruagaichean (Na *Grooa*-kichan,

The Maidens), the next Munro to the east. From here it continues up Stob Coire a' Chairn's broad, grassy south-east ridge, giving an easy 200m/650ft climb to the stony ▲summit.

The map for this route is combined with that for Am Bodach on Page 48.

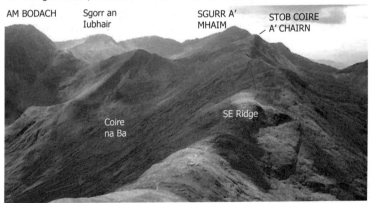

AM BODACH   Sgorr an
              Iubhair

SGURR A'   STOB COIRE
MHAIM   A' CHAIRN

Coire
na Ba

SE Ridge

▲An Gearanach 166 982m/3221ft (OS 41, NN 187669)

An Gyarranach, literally The Sad or Querulous One, but more likely The Short Ridge (from Gaelic Gearr Aonach)

AN GEARANACH   An Garbhanach

Viewed from Stob Coire a' Chairn

Viewed from Stob Coire a' Chairn to the south, An Gearanach appears as little more than the end point of the sharp summit ridge of its satellite Top, An Garbhanach (*An Garravanach*, The Rough Place). Viewed from Ben Nevis to the north, its true shape can be better appreciated, with steep, craggy northern slopes scalloped by a small corrie (Coire Chadha Chaoruinn, *Corra Chah-a Cheurin*, Rowan Pass Corrie,

unnamed on OS 1:50,000 map).

At first sight it might appear that an approach from this side would be every bit as exciting as that from An Garbhanach, but once again those nice path-building stalkers have manufactured a non-scramblers' route to the summit. Unlike the paths up the adjacent Munros of Am Bodach and Stob Coire a' Chairn, An Gearanach's path therefore begins on the north side of the mountains in Glen Nevis.

At the head of Glen Nevis, the great mountain ranges to the north (the Nevis Range) and the south (the Mamores) close in to form the Nevis Gorge, a deep ravine where the combination of crags, mixed woodland and rushing waters give it an almost Himalayan character (admittedly, on a somewhat smaller scale).

The route to An Gearanach begins with a walk through the gorge and is the most outstanding approach walk in the Central Highlands. It leads to a hidden mountain sanctuary where 110m/350ft An Steall (*An Shtyowl*, The Waterfall), the third highest waterfall in Scotland, tumbles onto a serene grassy plain.

An Gearanach from Glen Nevis
NN 168691, 6ml/10km, 850m/2790ft

The route begins at the car park at the end of the Glen Nevis road. In summer it is advisable to arrive early if you intend to park, otherwise the day will begin with a tiresome road walk from further down the glen.

At 460m/1500ft, this is the longest waterslide in the UK

In the Nevis Gorge

A renovated path, sometimes carved out of the rock, runs the whole length of the Nevis Gorge high above the Water of Nevis. The foaming torrent drops steeply from the plain at its head and is known as Eas an Tuill (*Ess an Too-il*, Waterfall of the Hole). As you progress it rises to meet the path, bringing you ever closer to its enormous water-worn boulders and potholes gouged out of the flanking rock walls.

The path through the gorge is little more than a rocky promenade, although you'll probably want to use hands for balance in places, especially when the path crosses polished or wet slabs above considerable drops. All

The rocky path through the Nevis Gorge

and sundry make their way up here in summer in all manner of footwear, but accidents happen, so take heed of any warning signs.

You emerge from the gorge onto the Plain of Steall, where the Water of Nevis flows peacefully between grassy haughs beneath An Steall, which tumbles down from Coire a' Mhail (*Corra Vaa-il*, Corrie of Rent) – a truly spectacular sight in full flow.

AN GEARANACH

Coire Chadha Chaoruinn

An Steall

Exiting the Nevis Gorge

To reach An Gearanach, it is necessary to cross the Water of Nevis and the side stream that flows into it from the waterfall. Across the Water of Nevis stands Steall climbers' hut, a private building reached by a notorious wire bridge of three strands: one double cable for the feet and higher single cables on each side for the hands. If you refuse to cross that

(and you won't be alone) you'll have to ford the river.

The shallowest crossing places, normally requiring no more than a watersplash or paddle, are just upriver from the bridge, at the confluence with the Steall stream, or further upriver, just beyond the waterfall. If you cross the bridge, you'll still have to cross the Steall stream, which can normally be

The high-wire act

done dryshod on boulders where the stream divides around a small island.

Beyond the waterfall, follow the path to the next stream along, which comes down from Coire Chadha Chaoruinn. Once across this stream (an easy crossing), the path turns right (south) to climb up the corrie, first on the left of the stream, then on the right. In

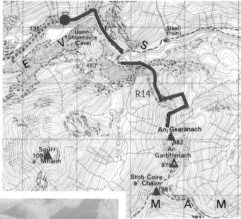

places this particular stalkers' path is rougher than some of its ilk but it gets the job done with a minimum of fuss. A short distance up, note the landslip that has carried part of the path away.

Higher up, when the angle steepens, zigzags ease the going as the path climbs towards cliffs at the head of the corrie. Before it reaches them, it takes a long dog-leg left, then back right, to cut beneath the rocks and exit the corrie onto its north-west rim. With expanding views, the path climbs more roughly up the corrie rim to end on An Gearanach's north shoulder, from where a worn path soon puts you at the ▲summit.

Beyond the summit of An Gearanach the ridge continues to An Garbhanach. This satellite Top looks temptingly close but one look will tell you it ain't gonna be so easy to reach. The ridge is broad and easy enough as far as the intervening dip but narrows beyond there and involves some scrambling. Nearing the summit, you'll especially remember one short, easy but exposed slab above a big drop on the right.

The walk through the Nevis Gorge to Steall and back makes a superb jaunt before afternoon cappuccino at a Glen Nevis watering hole. Or go in the evening, when the westering sun illuminates the spray from An Steall between flanking buttresses of shining quartzite. Go when rain pumps up the volume, or the spring, when the waters are swollen with snowmelt. Go again in autumn, when the birches are golden and the rowans heavy with red berries. Return trip: 2ml/3km, 80m/250ft.

▲Binnein Mor 27 1130m/3707ft (OS 41, NN 212663)
Beenyan Moar, Big Peak

Upper Glen Nevis

The four eastern Mamore Munros (Binnein Mor, Binnein Beag, Sgurr Eilde Mor and Na Gruagaichean) are challenging mountains far from the fleshpots of Glen Nevis, and their abrupt summits are awkward objectives for anyone with an aversion to loose rock. Binnein Mor is the highest and fittingly most striking Mamore of all, with a narrow summit ridge that tapers to an airy point.

Admirably, it adds to its attractiveness by taking compassion on non-scramblers and offering one easy route to its summit. For that we have to thank an excellent stalker's path that begins at Kinlochleven to the south and climbs all the way to the nearby Top of Sgor Eilde Beag (*Skor Ailtya Bake*, Little Peak of the Hinds). From here an easy ridge climbs to Binnein's South Top and summit.

Viewed from Sgurr a' Mhaim

Binnein Mor from Mamore Lodge (Kinlochleven)
NN 186629, 9ml/14km, 1070m/3500ft

From Mamore Lodge (see Page 46 for access) take the Land Rover track that climbs gently eastwards around the southern flanks of Na Gruagaichean. Nearing its high point, just before a left-hand bend, leave the track at NN 208635 (cairn) for the stalkers' path that branches left across the moor above Loch Eilde Mor. Ahead now is Sgor Eilde Beag, oddly a Top of Binnein Mor rather than Sgurr Eilde Mor, the next Munro to the east.

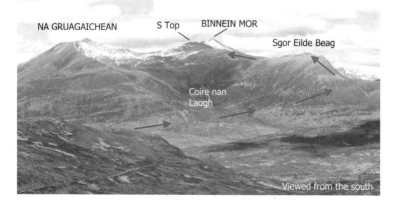

Viewed from the south

Sgor Eilde Beag

The big green corrie on the left, between Na Gruagaichean and Binnein Mor, is Coire nan Laogh (*Corra nan Leu*, Calf Corrie, unnamed on OS 1:50,000 map). After crossing its stream, the path climbs more steeply across Sgor Eilde Beag's south-east shoulder to the saddle between it and Sgurr Eilde Mor. On approach to the saddle, a cairn marks the spot where the main path zigzags left while an earthy short cut carries straight on. Stick to the main path.

Just after the path starts to level off onto the saddle, at a second cairned fork, branch left on another excellent stalker's path that zigzags up Sgor Eilde Beag's shoulder to its cliff-edge Δsummit. This is a fine perch above the large lochan on the saddle and an excellent spot from which to contemplate the skyline ahead, where the Mamore spine runs from Na Gruagaichean to Binnein Mor's ΔSouth Top, and from there along its south ridge to its tapering summit.

The spine is now easily reached. After a brief, stony descent to a shallow saddle, grassy slopes climb a broad shoulder to the ΔSouth Top.

SGURR EILDE MOR

Sgor Eilde Beag

Binnein Mor S Top

BINNEIN MOR

S Ridge

S Top

Sgor Eilde Beag

Viewed from Na Gruagaichean

Turning right to Binnein Mor's summit, you now traverse a section of ridge that, except for those who pine for some rock beneath their fingers, gives the perfect ridge walk. The crest is narrow enough to induce sensations of spaciousness, yet progress along it involves nothing harder than a walk along a path among the grass and boulders.

The ▲summit itself is an airy spot with steep drops to east and west, which heighten the northern view over upper Glen Nevis to Ben Nevis and the Grey Corries. If you fancy a brief scramble, a narrow little ridge, crested by boulders, continues northwards for a short distance before dropping to the moor.

After taking in your fill of the view, return by the route of ascent over the South Top and Sgor Eilde Beag.

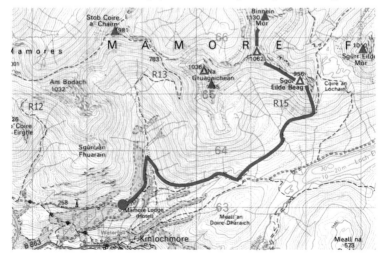

On the map, a return from Binnein Mor's South Top to Mamore Lodge via Na Gruagaichean's twin summits and the path down Coire na Ba (Route 13) looks short and attractive, but the traverse of the gap between the twin summits is a very exposed and loose scramble.

As the nearer twin is the Munro, you could bag it and return to the South Top, but even this is no route for sensitive souls. After crossing the intervening bealach, the connecting ridge from the South Top narrows to become a shattered arête. A path stays left at first to avoid the crest then it returns to the skyline once the crest becomes easy enough to walk along again. A 100m/300ft ascent will then put you at Na Gruagaichean's rockpile summit.

▲83 Ben Nevis 1 1344m/4409ft (OS 41, NN 166712)

Meaning obscure. A 17th century map names the mountain Ben Novesh. An 18th century description refers to Beniviss. Possible meanings include: Ugly Mountain (from Gaelic *ni-mhaise*), Venomous Mountain (from Gaelic *neimh*), Heavenly Mountain (from Gaelic *neamh*), Mountain with Keen Atmosphere (from Gaelic *neamh*), Cloud-capped Mountain (from Gaelic *neamh-bhathais*), Terrible Mountain (from old Irish *neamheis*). Note also that *nieves* is Spanish for snows. It is also possible that the mountain is named for the glen.

The climbers' approach path to the North Face

Ben Nevis is some mountain. If you were going to choose a mountain that, as the highest in the land, was going to represent your country, you could do worse than choose the Ben*. For a start, it's a big mountain, not only because of its height, which almost pushes the summit up to the snowline for its latitude, but also because of its huge bulk. When viewed from sea-level at Fort William or in Glen Nevis, its massive dome-like appearance will leave you in no doubt as to the effort required to climb it.

The normal route (described here) is the Mountain Track, which winds its seemingly endless way up the enormous, convex hillside above Glen Nevis. But this is only half the story, because in reality the Ben is only a *half*-dome. On its hidden north side, fringing the deep bowl of Coire Leis (*Corra Laish*, Sheltered Corrie), is a

1ml/1½km-long, 600m/2000ft-high north face that has Alpine scale and presence. Here, where snow often lies all year round (or at least used to), are rock and ice climbs of world-wide significance. You'll get close-up views of the face from the summit plateau.

And there's more. The Ben is connected to the adjacent Munro of Carn Mor Dearg (*Carn Moar Jerrak*, Big Red Cairn) by a graceful arête, affectionately known as the CMD

Arête, that curves around the head of Coire Leis and gives a classic scramble.

In short, the Ben fittingly encapsulates every aspect of the Highland walking and climbing experience. Does size matter? Is biggest best? We'll let you decide. One thing's for sure: Respect is due.

* You are allowed to refer to the mountain in such familiar fashion only after you have climbed it.

We hope you have better weather than poet John Keats encountered when he climbed Ben Nevis in 1818. As he wrote wistfully in a sonnet he composed at the summit: 'I look into the chasms and a shroud vaprous doth hide them'. However, the conditions at least gave him pause to muse on human nature: 'Even so vague is man's sight of himself!'

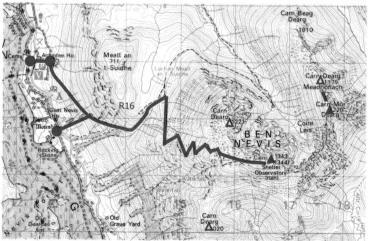

Glen Nevis Visitor Centre (NN 123728) is open daily 9-5 but opening hours are subject to change, especially out of season. Call 01397-705922 to verify.

The Roof of Britain

The earliest recorded ascents of Ben Nevis took place in the eighteenth century to aid research into developing sciences such as botany and geology. Interest in climbing the mountain for its own sake gathered pace only after the ascent was made easier a century later. In 1883 a meteorological observatory was built at the summit, together with a pony access track that is now the route taken by the Mountain Track.

In the early days the person who made most ascents was Clement Wragge. In the two years preceding the opening of the observatory, he climbed to the summit every day between June and October to take meteorological measurements. For the state in which this endeavour sometimes left him, he earned the nickname Inclement Rag.

The observatory was built to record 'the diversity of the mountain environment'. It operated from 1883 to 1904 and was later used as part of a summer 'hotel' that lasted until the end of the First World War.

In 2000 the summit area was purchased by the John Muir Trust and given a clean-up. Volunteers removed tons of litter and a clutter of personal memorials, which were replaced by a collective memorial built near a new Visitor Centre in Glen Nevis in 2006. Designated a Site for Contemplation, the memorial stands in the woods just beyond the north end of the car park.

All cairns except the summit cairn, a Peace Cairn war memorial and others used to aid navigation were removed. Uninformed visitors still erect more that have to be dismantled to prevent routefinding confusion.

The ruined walls of the observatory still stand. The remains of its tower are crowned by an emergency bivouac shelter, raised high (hopefully!) above winter snows. Despite the summer crowds that make it to the top, the summit remains a wild, remote and magical spot.

BEN NEVIS

CARN MOR DEARG

CMD Arête

Viewed from the south-east

Ben Nevis from Glen Nevis: The Mountain Track

9ml/14km, 1340m/4400ft Starting points: Visitor Centre (NN 123731),
Achintee (NN 126729), Youth Hostel (NN 128718)

This seemingly interminable manufactured highway to the heights isn't everyone's bowl of porridge. Pejoratively known as the 'Tourist Path', it has misled many a tourist into underestimating the effort required to ascend it.

Not only is Ben Nevis almost a Munro-and-a-half in height, but the ascent begins virtually at sea level. The height to be climbed is twice as much as on many inland Munros. Then there's the nature of the path – a 4½ml/7km ribbon of stone and rubble up a vast mountainside that is as tiring to descend as to ascend

and which hides the summit until the very last.

Without its switchbacks and staircases of rock and rubble, however, the track would become dangerously eroded (as it was before restoration) and unable to withstand the 160,000+ ascents it currently receives each year.

Although a prolonged slogathon, it does provide an easy way up the highest Munro of all, its completion engenders a rare feeling of accomplishment, and the summit is an amazing place whichever way you get there.

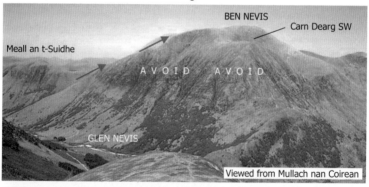

BEN NEVIS

Carn Dearg SW

Meall an t-Suidhe

A V O I D   A V O I D

GLEN NEVIS

Viewed from Mullach nan Coirean

After the main railway reached Fort William in 1894, there were plans to build a rack railway up Ben Nevis to service the newly built observatory. If it's good enough for the highest peak in Wales...

Anyone intent on reaching the summit by ascending the pony track, meanwhile, had to pay a fee: one shilling (5p) on foot,

three shillings (15p) on horseback and twenty-one shillings (105p) for hire of a pony and guide.

At the summit 'hotel' that replaced the observatory at the start of the twentieth century, lunch cost three shillings (15p) and an overnight stay cost ten shillings (50p). Now that's civilised.

Two views of the lower Mountain Track

Glen Nevis

Despite insufficient funding, the John Muir Trust continues to do sterling work on path restoration and environmental and visitor management. Tons of rubbish are removed from the mountain each year. To ensure the Ben's well-being for those who come after us, please do not erect cairns, leave personal memorials or add to the litter.

The track has three starting points. One begins at the Ben Nevis Inn, at the end of the short road to Achintee on the north side of the River Nevis. This is the time-honoured approach, following the line of the observatory pony track. A newer second approach begins across the River Nevis from Achintee, at a bridge near the Visitor Centre on the Glen Nevis road. The third approach begins a short distance further down the road at the bridge opposite the Youth Hostel.

Despite a small parking fee and the unavailability of refreshments (apart from a vending machine), the Visitor Centre, with extensive parking and toilet facilities, is the normal starting point nowadays. The path bridges the River Nevis at the north end of the car park and joins the Achintee path 120m beyond its start, adding negligible distance to the day.

The Ben Nevis Inn has free parking and refreshments. The YH path, from very limited roadside parking, climbs steeply up the hillside to join the main path at the 170m/550ft contour.

For directions we humbly suggest that you simply follow the person in front of you. But even if you find yourself in the newsworthy position of being the only person on the mountain, it would require negligence in the extreme to stray off-route on a clear day.

To add interest to an ascent of the Mountain Track, why not go for a record? The fastest time for the Ben Nevis Race, up and down from Claggan Park in Fort William, stands at under 1½ hours (that's right – one and a half hours).

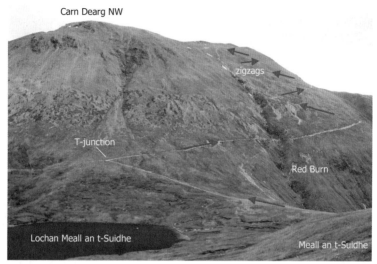

Carn Dearg NW

zigzags

T-junction

Red Burn

Lochan Meall an t-Suidhe

Meall an t-Suidhe

In its lower half, the track curves around the southern slopes of Meall an t-Suidhe (*Myowl an Tu-ya*, aka *Melon Tea*, Hill of the Seat), a hill top on the Ben's north-west flanks. The surface has been 'stabilised' to such an extent that it is more a rock staircase *cum* boulder hop than a path.

The angle eases as it climbs onto the saddle east of Meall an t-Suidhe, where Lochan Meall an t-Suidhe nestles beneath Carn Dearg North-west (*Carn Jerrak*, Red Cairn). At a height of 630m/2050ft on the saddle, a T-junction marks the approximate half-way point.

Meall an t-Suidhe

T-junction

Descending the zigzags

Carn Mòr Dearg

Carn Dearg 1221

Coire na h-Urchaire

Fords

Le chan o Ciste

Coire na Ciste

Coire Leis

Carn Mòr Dearg Arête

Glen Nevis

Path

1343 11344r Cairn

Shelter

Observatory (ruin)

Coire Ghaimhnean

Ben Nevis

Five Finger Gully Waterfall

● Bottom of zigzags
■ Top of zigzags, start of cairns

Detailed map of Ben Nevis summit at 2 x scale

The left branch here crosses the saddle to Coire Leis. The Mountain Track cuts back sharp right across the stony slopes of Carn Dearg to the Red Burn. This is the more common name for the Allt na h-Urchaire, which tumbles down from Coire na h-Urchaire (*Corra na Hoora-churra*, Corrie of the Shot) above.

Beyond the Red Burn the track reaches a sharp left-hand bend that marks a major turning point. Above here it deteriorates into a stony highway that zigzags up the Ben's north-west shoulder. As height is gained, views expand over Glen Nevis to the Mamores, but in reality you're likely to have eyes only for the next rubbly zig or zag and wonder if the summit will ever hove into sight.

Four major zigzags (follow the track left and right four times) take you up to a stone windbreak at the 1200m contour. Here the track turns left to begin the crossing of the wilderness of broken rock that forms the Roof of Britain. N.B. Ignore a side path that goes straight on above the depths of Five Finger Gully, which has claimed many lives.

MacLean's Steep

Navigation cairn

The Roof of Britain

A series of pyramid-shaped stone cairns, each 1.8m tall, now line the track at 50m intervals to aid foul-weather navigation. After 400m, and now less than 600m from the summit, you reach the last steepening, known as MacLean's Steep (for the local contractor who built the observatory). Cairns 8 to 11 take you up MacLean's Steep, then the remaining cairns veer right, away from the track (but useful when it is snow-covered).

Above MacLean's Steep, the track tops out on the Ben's summit plateau close to the edge of the north face. The ▲summit itself is now close at hand, seen across the rim of Gardyloo Gully, the north face's most deep-cut indentation. It is necessary to go around the rim of this gully to reach the summit plinth. If there is snow on the ground, give the rim a wide berth as its enormous cornice can be mistaken for solid ground. Take especial care in cloud. A triangle of three cairns beyond the lip marks the presence of solid ground.

After suitable R&R, pick your way back down the Mountain Track with care, especially the rocky lower half. Its unrelenting nature is such that, if you have dodgy knees, you can expect to have lost any remaining cartilage by the time you reach the glen.

Summit architecture

Emergency shelter

Observatory

Peace Cairn

Gardyloo Gully was the gully into which observatory staff tipped their rubbish. The name 'Gardyloo' is an Anglicisation of the French *Garde de l'eau*, meaning Beware of the Water.

▲**Aonach Mor** 8 1221m/4006ft (OS 41, NN 192729)
Ernach Moar, Big Ridge
▲**Aonach Beag** 7 1234m/4048ft (OS 41, NN 196715)
Ernach Bake, Little Ridge

The Back Corries
of the Aonachs

AONACH BEAG

AONACH MOR

An Cul Choire

Immediately east of Ben Nevis lie two more big mountains that would be better appreciated were it not for the commanding presence of the Ben. Their Cairngorm-like summit plateaus would certainly win no prizes in a beauty contest, yet they have immense presence and stand atop some colossal scenery. Interestingly, the Little Aonach is higher than the Big Aonach, probably because the mountains were named from below for their bulk rather than their height.

The two summits rim an imposing eastern wall, over 3ml/5km long, that rivals the Ben's north face for Alpine scale and grandeur. The cliffs are indented by a series of huge corries

named the Back Corries after the most outstanding of them – An Cul Choire (*An Cool Chorra*, The Back Corrie).

Access to Aonach Mor in particular has been revolutionised in recent years by the Nevis Range ski development in its north-west corrie (Coire an t-Sneachda, *Corran Trechka*, Snowy Corrie). The usual approach is now from the Nevis Range car park, using the gondola to gain 550m/1800ft of initial height and start the walk 650m/2150ft above sea-level. You may think that's cheating, but at the time of writing other approach options are limited as there is no dedicated path for walkers between the gondola's base station and top station.

Aonach Mor from Nevis Range car park NN 172774
Using gondola: 6ml/10km, 880m/2900ft
Avoiding gondola: 11ml/18km, 1430m/4700ft

The Nevis Range ski development is friendlier to mountain bikers than it is to hillwalkers. A purpose-built mountain bike trail, which has obliterated the former path, runs from the gondola top station to the car park, but at the time of writing its use by walkers is severely restricted.

During the biking season (mid-May to mid-September) walkers are allowed to use the trail only outside operational hours (around 9.30 to 18.00), which leaves little room for manoeuvre.

Eschewing the gondola, you can use forest tracks to reach open hillside under your own steam, but respect is due to anyone who has the motivation to do so. Make a note of the following directions anyway, in case the gondola is closed.

From the car park, follow forest tracks into the glen of the Allt Daim, aiming for the track-end at NN 167757. From here, climb to the ridge on the left, which separates the Allt Daim from Coire an t-Sneachda, then continue up to a bump on the ridge called Meall Beag (*Myowl Bake*, Little Hill, NN 178753, named only on OS 1:25,000 map). If using the gondola, a dirt road contours across Coire an t-Sneachda from the top station to Meall Beag.

Nevis Range information. The gondola runs all year round, except mid-November to mid-December, when it is closed for annual maintenance. During the skiing season it runs from 9.00 (8.30 at weekends) to dusk (around 16.00). During July and August it runs from 9.30 to 18.00. At other times it runs from 10.00 to 17.00. In winter a chairlift can be used to gain more height. Verify this information and view a webcam at www.nevisrange.co.uk or call 01397-705825.

GiGi: Coire an t-Sneachda's spring snowfield melts into the shape of a goose, hence the name of the top station restaurant.

AONACH MOR summit plateau

Above Meall Beag the broad ridge forms the corrie's west-bounding rim and gives an easy ascent to Aonach Mor's summit plateau. With height, a path becomes increasingly distinct on grass among boulders. At a height of 1100m/3600ft (NN 188741) you'll reach a ski tow and associated snow fencing that can be followed all the way up to the plateau. The tow tops out right at the rim of the east face above Coire an Lochain, the first of the Back Corries.

N.B. From the dirt road that crosses Coire an t-Sneachda from the gondola top station, it is possible to take a short cut up to the ridge to avoid the dog-leg via Meall Beag, but any line (even on traces of paths) is likely to enmesh you in bog and snow fencing.

AONACH MOR

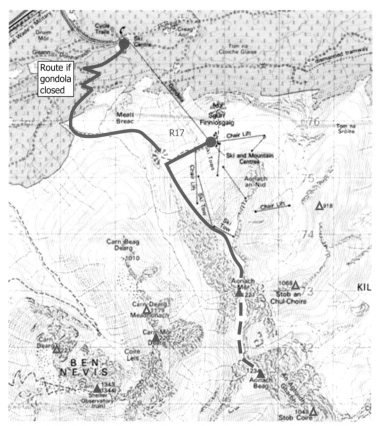

Aonach Mor's tundra-like summit plateau is virtually level for hundreds of metres. Simply follow the cliff edge or take a more direct line to reach the ▲summit cairn, set 100m back from the edge.

On descent remember that, if the gondola is closed, you are allowed to use the mountain biking path. On World Cup days, expert cyclists hurtle down here in under five minutes, but you are likely to take a tad longer.

As on the best Alpine walks, you can obtain refreshment at the foot of the mountain in the Pinemarten Coffee Shop and half-way up (and down) at the gondola top station in the Snowgoose Restaurant, where there's also a shop and a mountain discovery centre. Don't forget to carry some cash with you.

Bonus Munro: Aonach Beag add-on return: 2ml/3km, 290m/950ft

AONACH MOR

AONACH BEAG

Continuing to Aonach Beag on mossy terrain, an earthy path descends gently from Aonach Mor's summit to the intervening 1080m/3550ft saddle, rimming the vast hollow of An Cul Choire. The corrie's huge crags rise to Aonach Beag's summit and a path picks out the easiest line up steep slopes of rock and rubble beside them. N.B. There's a brief section at the start where you may use hands to aid uplift. Above here, easy ground returns for the short walk onto ▲Aonach Beag's bare summit dome.

To descend, reverse the route over Aonach Mor.

AONACH BEAG

An Cul Choire

AONACH MOR

▲Stob Ban 178 977m/3205ft (OS 41, NN 266723)
Stop Baan, White Mountain, named for its quartzite cap

E Ridge

STOB BAN

East of Ben Nevis and the Aonachs, there is a dramatic change in the character of the mountains as massive plateau summits give way to sharp-pointed peaks, linked by a slender 5ml/8km-long ridge. The mountains are collectively known as the Grey Corries on account of the pale quartzite slopes that give them their characteristic appearance when seen from afar.

The main spine boasts no less than three Munros and six Tops, which give outstanding ridge walking and easy scrambling to rival anything on the nearby Mamores. Lateral ridges to the north sport a further two Tops, while a deep bealach to the south isolates a fourth Munro – Stob Ban.

Stob Ban, not to be confused with its namesake in the Mamores, is an idiosyncratic Munro with multiple personalities. Viewed from Lagganside, its summit cone dominates its surroundings, making it one of the most recognisable peaks in the Central Highlands.

The northern flanks harbour the rock tiers of the Giant's Staircase, which aspires to be the best scramble in the Grey Corries. On the other hand, that summit cone, like that of its Mamores namesake, is one big contrasting heap of quartzite rubble.

In short, Stob Ban is a quirky peak that constantly surprises. Thanks to a grassy east/north-east ridge, it is much the easiest Grey Corries Munro to climb and its summit rewards with a commanding view.

Stob Ban from Coirechoille (Glen Spean)
NN 256788, 11ml/17km, 850m/2800ft

The route begins near Coirechoille Lodge, at the end of the 2½ml/ 4km minor road on the south side of the River Spean east of Spean Bridge. There is no parking at the end of the paved road (NN 252807) but a rough Land Rover track on the right, open to the public and passable for most road vehicles, climbs past the lodge to give closer access to the mountains.

If you don't wish to drive the track you'll have to park a long way back and add considerable mileage to the route. With care, drive c.1½ml/2km up the track to a small car park just before a forestry plantation.

Stob Coire na Ceannain   GREY CORRIES

STOB COIRE CLAURIGH

Lairig Leacach

From the car park, walk 1ml/1½km along the continuing Land Rover track through the plantation to a gate at its upper end. From here, the track continues around the eastern foot of the Grey Corries through the ancient hill pass of the Lairig Leacach (*Lahrik Lyech-kach*, Slabby or Granite Pass).

It is 4ml/6km to the foot of the mountain and the same distance back at the end of the day, but it is an easy, scenic walk that takes you to the heart of remote country. Relax and savour. Above the upper forest boundary, the track crosses the river and rises very gently to the summit of the lairig, gaining only 140m/450ft in 2ml/3km. The pass is so gentle that you'll have difficulty spotting its highpoint.

Over the summit, the track descends slightly into a broad green valley. A corner is rounded and Stob Ban bursts into view at last. It's hard

to believe that the soaring, conical summit is only 500m/1650ft above. A little further along, the track rounds another corner and reaches an open bothy, superbly sited at the foot of the mountain's north-east ridge.

Beyond the bothy the route crosses a stream (stepping stones or bridge just upstream) and follows the continuing path through the Lairig Leacach. After a couple of hundred metres the path splits at a Y-fork. Take the right branch to climb the north-east ridge.

Incorrigibly, the path goes straight up the rocky hump seen ahead before continuing less steeply up a shallow depression right of the skyline (this latter section can become quite boggy after rain). At the top of the depression the path emerges onto a shoulder,

STOB BAN

from where there are great views both of the pyramid summit and the Giant's Staircase in the corrie below (see next page).

(see next page)

The ridge now veers left and the path follows it, traversing the hillside below (right of) the crest to bypass a minor rise and reach the saddle beyond. The ridge then veers right again, becoming the east ridge, and rears steeply upwards. The path climbs grassy slopes to a small levelling, beyond which you are faced with the final 150m/500ft summit pyramid of quartzite shale.

Fortunately, the going isn't as tiresome as it looks. The stony path zigzags up without causing too many retrograde steps and you'll soon be at the ▲summit admiring the panoramic view.

At the head of Coire Claurigh behind the Lairig Leacach bothy, tier upon tier of beautifully clean quartzite slabs rise to the bealach at the foot of Stob Ban's north ridge, between Stob Ban and Stob Choire Claurigh. The slabs form a series of rock steps known as the Giant's Staircase... scramblers for the enjoyment of.

On the map a return from Stob Ban over the neighbouring Munro of Stob Choire Claurigh (*Stop Chorra Clowry*, meaning obscure) looks tempting, but it would involve the descent of loose quartzite chippings on Stob Ban's very steep north ridge and the traverse of a very narrow and exposed rock ridge at Claurigh's summit.

▲Beinn na Lap 241 935m/3068ft (OS 41, NN 376695)
Ben na Laap, Dappled Mountain

BEINN NA LAP

Corrour

Loch Ossian

Beinn na Lap is the isolated highpoint on a long ridge that runs beside remote Loch Ossian. It is the furthest Munro from any road and would be out of reach as a day walk were it not for the existence of nearby Corrour Station on the West Highland Railway. It is the only mountain in the Highlands that requires a train journey to its foot.

Situated at a height of 410m/1307ft on Rannoch Moor, Corrour lies in the middle of a 50ml/80km-wide expanse of roadless land that stretches from the west coast to the Cairngorms. Despite the presence of the railway, estate tracks and sporadic buildings, it feels like wilderness. The main hazard here is agoraphobia. When the train

departs and leaves you stranded on the platform, you may experience a frisson of misgiving over what you have let yourself in for.

In shape Beinn na Lap resembles an enormous unrepentant pimple with two of its sides squeezed together. From Corrour, the whole ascent route is in view – a straightforward tramp up uniform slopes from lochside to summit, with zero features of interest beside the scenery. But what scenery!

The mountain's supreme location generates a tremendous sense of being at the heart of wilderness and gives plenty of reason to pause on ascent to ponder the nature of existence. Just hope there isn't a rail strike while you're up there.

The train runs between Glasgow and Fort William. From the south, drive to Crianlarich, Tyndrum or Bridge of Orchy and board it there. From the north, board it at Tulloch in Glen Spean.

From Monday to Saturday the railway timetable usually allows around seven hours at Corrour between arrival and departure (c.11.30 to c.18.30 from the south, c.8.30 to c.15.30 from the north). On Sundays there are no useful trains for day trips. For up-to-date timetable information, visit www.scotrail.co.uk or call 0845-6015929.

Beinn na Lap from Corrour Station
NN 356664, 6ml/10km, 550m/1800ft

From Corrour Station, take the Land Rover track to Loch Ossian. When the track forks to encircle the loch, go left for a few hundred metres to another fork (NN 366671). Walk up the left branch, signposted 'Loch Treig Road to the Isles', for c.50m, to the first left-hand bend.

The obvious boot-worn path up Beinn na Lap begins here and makes a beeline up the hillside to the skyline of the south-west ridge. It is boggy in places and steepens higher up but, with a cheerful disposition and well-timed pauses to admire the scenery, you should reach the skyline with a minimum of fuss.

Once on the south-west ridge, which is optimistically named Ceann Caol (*Kyann Keul*, Narrow Head) on the map, the going and the views improve dramatically. The ridge rises at a gentle angle, surfaced by grass and broken rocks on which a developing path is trying to gain purchase. The ascent tops out on a small, gently sloping summit plateau, with a small rise at the near end, beyond which a tiny lochan separates you from the ▲summit.

Ascent to the SW Ridge

On the SW Ridge

BEINN NA LAP

Summit plateau and lochan

Corrour Station House, leased from Corrour estate by the Scottish Youth Hostels Association in 2010, has accommodation and serves refreshments. For up-to-date information on opening times call direct (01397-732-236) or contact SYHA (website: www.syha.org.uk, tel: 0845-2937373).

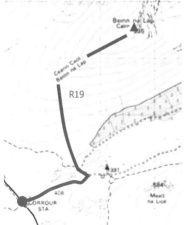

For a scenic wilderness taster, try a between-trains stroll around Loch Ossian, which lies just east of Corrour Station (9ml/14km on a Land Rover track).

Spring and autumn at Loch Ossian are exceptionally colourful. Go a-wanderin' in spring to catch the rhododendrons in full bloom, or in autumn to see the sycamores blaze with colour.

▲Sgairneach Mhor 155 991m/3251ft (OS 42, NN 598731)
Scarnyach Voar, Big Stony Place
▲Beinn Udlamain 119 1011m/3317ft (OS 42, NN 579739)
Ben Ootlaman, obscure, often translated as Joint or Unsteady
Mountain (from Gaelic *Udalan*, meaning a Swivel Joint), but a more
appropriate derivation may be from Gaelic *Udlaidh*, meaning Gloomy

A' MHARCONAICH

Drumochter   The Boar
Pass   SGAIRNEACH MHOR

Squeezed between Loch Ericht and Drumochter Pass on the A9, a triangle of nondescript country forms the Central Highlands' loneliest outpost. At first sight, the four Munros here seem to be lacklustre lumps that are half-hidden behind the even duller humps of the Sow of Atholl and the Boar of Badenoch.

Their convex forms, dull colour, featureless hillsides and encircling moors do little to enthuse. The road and railway are in sight and earshot on all ascents, and the giant electricity pylons that march through the pass add nothing to the ambience.

Now for the good news. Thanks to the 452m/1483ft height reached by the road, you get a maximum of Munro for a minimum of effort in these parts. Moreover, once on the skyline, plateau summits and broad ridges,

characterised by gentle angles and easy terrain, do much to compensate for the mountains' indifferent welcome.

Sgairneach Mhor and its neighbour Beinn Udlamain lie at the head of Coire Dhomhain (*Corra Ghoe-in*, Deep Corrie), the long defile that cuts into the hills between the Sow and the Boar. Although the roadside prospect does little to inspire, to say nothing of the mountains' Gaelic names, there are worse things to do in life than stride out along their ridge tops. Moreover, a Land Rover track up the corrie gives an easy approach through the heathery drumlins at its mouth to give ready access to the heights.

Go on a sunny day, without expectations, and you may well find yourself enjoying a strangely Tolerable Traipse across the Tops.

Sgairneach Mhor from Coire Dhomhain (A9)
NN 632756, 6ml/10km, 550m/1800ft

Begin at the lay-by on the A9 at the mouth of the corrie. The Land Rover track up the corrie begins on the far side of the railway line and is reached by a railway underpass. This will be found by walking a few hundred metres south along the old road that runs parallel to the A9. At the first stream south of the lay-by, a path takes a short cut, but following it would involve crossing (i.e. trespassing on) the railway line.

SGAIRNEACH MHOR

Coire Creagach

BEINN UDLAMAIN →

Coire Dhomhain

Walk up the undulating corrie track past the Sow, going further than you might expect, until you reach a small trackside cairn (NN 615750). Don't miss this. Take the path that descends from here to cross the Allt Coire Dhomhain. You may have to de-boot to paddle across.

The Boar

The Sow

A9

Coire Dhomhain

Looking back down the ascent route

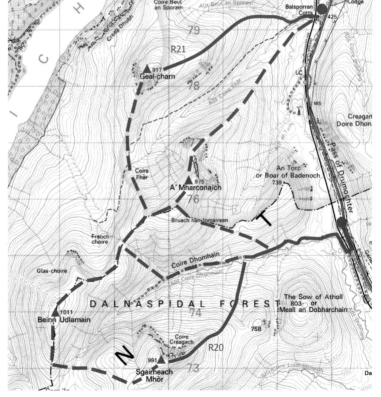

On the far side of the river a path climbs the uniform, gentle, heathery hillside on the right-hand (west) bank of the stream that comes down from the saddle between Point 758 and Sgairneach Mhor. From below, this is seen as a dip on Sgairneach Mhor's north-east ridge, west of the deeper bealach that separates Point 758 from the Sow.

The path will be springy if you're lucky, boggy if you're not. Higher up, it bears right beside a streamlet to reach the crest of the north-east ridge some way above the dip. If you lose it, head for the ridge to pick up an ATV track that climbs the crest. Path and track join to continue up gentle slopes of rock-strewn turf to a small, cairned rise at the rim of Coire Creagach (*Corra Craikach*, Craggy Corrie), for which the mountain may be named. Sgairneach Mhor's ▲summit lies a short distance away around the rim.

Bonus Munro: Beinn Udlamain add-on 3ml/5km, 200m/650ft

Beinn Udlamain is an easy bonus Munro whose ascent turns the route into a round trip. From Sgairneach Mhor a twisting descent follows the lie of the land south-west, then north-west, then south-west again, to the 809m/ 2655ft bealach at the head of Coire Dhomhain. You should come across a path that crosses the right-hand edge of the peaty bealach. Good going makes the path redundant on descent, but it proves useful on the rougher ascent to Udlamain's stonier south ridge. Once on the ridge, with views opening up across Loch Ericht to Ben Alder, follow a line of old fence posts past a stone shelter to the plateau ▲summit.

BEINN UDLAMAIN

SGAIRNEACH MHOR

Traffic Scotland maintains real-time CCTV cameras facing both north and south along the A9 at Drumochter Pass, and these can be accessed to obtain current weather information. View live images at www.trafficscotland.org/lev/index.aspx.

BEN ALDER

Loch Ericht

The view from Beinn Udlamain

Over the summit, the broad ridge continues north-eastwards, back towards the A9, with perfect turf going and an excellent path. Still following the fence posts, it twists gently down over a couple of rises and reaches the 861m/2825ft bealach before A' Mharconaich. This third Munro is often climbed together with Geal-charn (see opposite), but you can also bag it from here (see below), otherwise descend into Coire Dhomhain .

The track back down the corrie lies only 250m/800ft below and is easily reached by descending well right of the main stream. In order to find the least steep and least heathery line down, plan the descent route from across the corrie while you're at the summit of Sgairneach Mhor.

A' MHARCONAICH

Bealach

BEINN UDLAMAIN

From the bealach before A' Mharconaich the ascent to the summit tempts with a height gain of only 120m/400ft. The summit plateau consists of two rounded tops separated by a shallow saddle. The first top reached is the south-west top. The line of fence posts from Beinn Udlamain descends south-east from here, following the boundary line shown on the OS map. The second top (the north-east top at the rim of the eastern corrie) sports two cairns. The second cairn marks the true ▲summit.

Return to the south-west top and descend from there to the Coire Dhomhain track, following the fence posts and seeking grassy patches in the heather.

▲**Geal-charn** 279 917m/3008ft (OS 42, NN 598731)
Gyal Charn, White Cairn
▲▲**A' Mharconaich** 179 975m/3199ft (OS 42, NN 604762)
A Varkanich, The Place of Horses

GEAL-CHARN

Balsporran
Cottages

Immediately north of Sgairneach Mhor and Beinn Udlamain (Route 20), these two Drumochter Pass Munros form the highpoints on either side of Coire Fhar (poss. meaning Winding Corrie). This is another long, nondescript defile that runs parallel to neighbouring Coire Dhomhain.

As befitting the general tenor of the area (see description on Page 82), Geal-charn is the lowest of four Central Highland Munros that bear that name and its summit is the most easily reached on the whole of the A9. As in Coire Dhomhain, a good track climbs Coire Fhar and from it another heads up Geal-charn's north-east ridge on increasingly easy-angled terrain.

On the other side of Coire Fhar, A' Mharconaich looks more exciting from the roadside, with a high eastern corrie whose well-defined rim suggests a narrower ridge walk than might be expected hereabouts. In reality the ridge turns out to be just as broad as all the others.

To extend the day after the short trip up Geal-charn, you can continue around the head of Coire Fhar and bag A' Mharconaich as a bonus Munro while you've got your boots on.

GEAL-CHARN

A' Mharconaich

Viewed from Beinn Udlamain

Geal-charn from Balsporran Cottages (A9)
NN 628792, 5ml/8km, 490m/1600ft

To match the Land Rover track up Coire Dhomhain, a good ATV track climbs to the head of Coire Fhar, giving easy access to the heights. From the car park at Balsporran Cottages (former railway cottages), follow the track across the railway line and up the corrie for a few hundred metres, to the Allt Beul an Sporain (*Owlt Bay-ul an Sporran*,

GEAL-CHARN

anglicised to Balsporran, Stream of the Mouth of the Sporran or Pouch).

Subsidiary ATV tracks branch right to climb the hillside on both sides of the stream. Ignore the first branch (on the near side of the stream), follow the main track across the bridged stream, then take the next branch,

about 130m beyond the bridge. The track climbs onto the broad, gentle north-east ridge of Geal-charn and gives an easy ascent.

The going is boggy at first but improves with height as the track becomes a broad path across heathy terrain. After reaching a rounded rise,

Nearing the summit

GEAL-CHARN

the path becomes less distinct on ever more gentle slopes that continue to the flat, twin-cairned, bouldery summit plateau. The far cairn marks the ▲summit, where the view west opens up across Loch Ericht to the Ben Alder group.

The map for this route is combined with that for neighbouring Sgairneach Mhor on Page 84.

Bonus Munro: A' Mharconaich add-on 3ml/5km, 240m/800ft

Continuing to A' Mharconaich from Geal-charn adds a fair amount of effort to the day but is perfectly feasible. Leaving Geal-charn's summit, bouldery ground persists on the descent, south-west then south, to the 739m/2425ft bealach below A' Mharconaich at the head of Coire Fhar. Despite the rocky terrain, the ridge is broad and gentle, which makes for an easy descent. On the way down you'll pick up a path and then rejoin the upper Coire Fhar ATV track, which continues to the bealach.

At the low point of the bealach there's a fork. The main track continues right, to traverse the hillside into Fraoch-choire (*Freuch Coire*, Heather Corrie) below Beinn Udlamain. Leave it to branch left on a rougher path that climbs steeper slopes of

rocks and heath. The path becomes indistinct as the angle eases onto the south-west ridge of A' Mharconaich, but you can gain the skyline easily at any point.

Once up, a short and speedy trip along the grassy ridge brings you to A' Mharconaich's summit plateau. As noted on Page 86, the ▲summit is the second top reached, beyond a shallow saddle, at the far end of the plateau.

To descend, go left (north) around the rim of the eastern corrie. After an initial steep descent on stony ground, the going eases as the ridge curves right above Coire Fhar. A path leads down the ridge and crosses the boggy moor at its foot, staying on the right side of the Allt Coire Fhar all the way to the railway bridge at Balsporran Cottages.

A' MHARCONAICH

Balsporran
Cottages ▴

▲Beinn a' Chaorainn 80 1052m/3453ft (OS 34, NN 386851)

Ben a Cheurin, Mountain of the Rowan

BEINN TEALLACH

BEINN A' CHAORAINN

R23

R22

Viewed from across Glen Spean

Between the A9 at Dalwhinnie/ Kingussie and the west coast at Fort William/Spean Bridge, the A86 runs alongside Loch Laggan reservoir and through Glen Spean, bisecting the Central Highlands from east to west.

On the south side of the road three Munros form the Ardverikie Trio (Route 24), while on the north side of the road another three form the Creag Meaghaidh massif (Route 25). West of these the retiring summits of Beinn a' Chaorainn (described here) and Beinn Teallach (Route 23) offer less compelling mountainscapes when viewed from the roadside, but appearances are deceptive. Their nondescript southern slopes give easy ascent routes to scenic summits.

Beinn a' Chaorainn in particular is a triple-topped, deeply ice-gouged peak that harbours two great eastern corries. They can't match Coire Ardair of Creag Meaghaidh in stature but they do boast a cliff-edge rim walk and a rocky spur (the east ridge) that separates them. The climb up the east ridge is a classic scramble and you'll get good views of it and the corries from the easy route to the summit.

With three highpoints of similar elevation, Beinn a' Chaorainn's summit plateau has been a source of considerable trouble for Munro's Tables over the years. Both current summit (Centre Top) and South Top were listed at 1049m in the 1997 Tables.

Prior to then, between 1974 and 1997, the Centre Top was listed at 1052m, and this is currently the case again on OS maps. It has been suggested that cornice formation may contribute to differing height measurements.

In Tables history, the South Top was the Munro between 1891 and 1974. The Centre Top was a Top in 1891, was deleted from the Tables completely in 1921(!) and was reinstated as the Munro in 1974, which it has been ever since. Maybe you should climb both tops, and the North Top as well (1043m, see Page 93) just in case.

Beinn a' Chaorainn from Roughburn (Glen Spean)
NN 377814, 6ml/10km, 850m/2800ft

Begin at the car park at the bridge over the Allt a' Chaorainn near Roughburn on the A86, just east of Laggan Dam. Take the forest track into the trees and, c.200m beyond a sharp right-hand bend, branch left at a fork. N.B. Ignore the path and the forest break on the bend itself.

Around 100m along the left branch, a cairn marks the start of a boggy path that tunnels up a forest break to reach open ground at a stile. The arboreal quagmire at the start can be avoided among the trees on the right.

BEINN A' CHAORAINN
S Top
Meall Clachaig
SW Ridge
BEINN TEALLACH

Above the forest, Chaorainn's broad south-west ridge climbs all the way to the South Top, although at first the crags of Meall Clachaig (*Myowl Clachak*, Rocky Hill) block the way. Paths fork left and right at the stile. To avoid rocky ground, take the left-hand path, even though it contours further left than seems warranted before turning to find a way up the hillside.

It is not the driest of paths and may be difficult to follow in places, but it is infinitely less tiresome than the heather on either side. It stays below the crest of the ridge until petering out on approach to a level section behind Meall Clachaig (NN 375835). Note this spot for the return trip.

Now on the broad ridge crest, another indistinct path leads onwards and upwards. The top seen ahead is only a shoulder of the mountain but the South Top isn't far beyond. As height is gained, more and more rocks litter the hillside. The path is reduced to traces then gives up altogether, but the going remains good on grass and turf among the rocks.

At the ΔSouth Top, with the main effort now behind you, you can relax and enjoy your reward – the broad, scenic ridge walk around the rim of the two eastern corries.

Beyond the South Top, the ridge rims the first of the corries and gives good views of the east ridge (its far bounding rim). The corrie is named Coire Ban (*Corra Bahn*, White Corrie) for its foaming stream.

Beinn a' Chaorainn's ▲summit (Centre Top) is perched at the top of the east ridge, overlooking the second, even grander corrie.

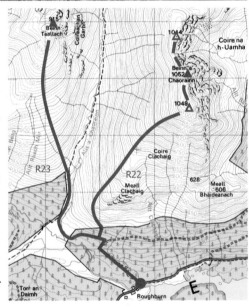

Bonus Top: North Top add-on return 1ml/1½km, 90m/300ft

The second great eastern corrie of Beinn a' Chaorainn comes complete with lochan and is named Coire na h-Uamha (*Corra na Hoo-aha*, Corrie of the Cave) for a cave at NN 400820, just above the roadside waterfall marked on the OS map.

The short, scenic, sky-high stroll to the ∆North Top, along a narrowing grassy ridge above the corrie depths, is just recompense on its own for the effort of the ascent to the summit.

BEINN A' CHAORAINN

N Top

Coire na h-Uamha

Viewed from the summit

Beinn a' Chaorainn is separated from its neighbour Beinn Teallach by the glen of the Allt a' Chaorainn, whose head forms a deep 614m/2015ft bealach between them. The bealach is one humongous, wet, sprawling hollow. It is possible to cross it and fashion a joint bagging expedition but it is more congenial to climb each peak on its own.

S Top   BEINN A' CHAORAINN

Summit   E Ridge

N Top

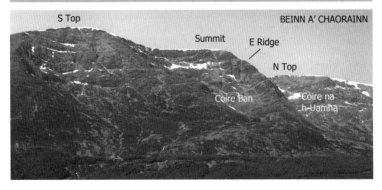

Coire Ban   Coire na h-Uamha

▲Beinn Teallach 283 914m/3000ft (OS 34 or 41, NN 361859)
Ben Tyallach, Mountain of the Forge or Fireplace, perhaps named for the appearance of its steep eastern corries

BEINN TEALLACH

Allt a' Chaorainn

U nlike its near namesake, the redoubtable An Teallach in the Northern Highlands, Beinn Teallach is conspicuously lacking in dramatic scenery. Let's face it, if future geological re-alignment resulted in its diminution by a mere foot, it would be no great loss to the Tables. Approached by its south ridge from the A86, it is little more than a big wet heap of a hill that will thoroughly test the waterproofness of your boots.

That said, it is an easy Munro to climb. The elevation gain is 120m/ 400ft less than on neighbouring Beinn

a' Chaorainn (Route 22) and an ATV track up the south ridge further reduces the effort involved. At the summit you'll overlook steep eastern and northern corries that give the mountain more definition than when viewed from the roadside: Coireachan Garbh (*Corrachan Garrav*, Rough Corries) and Coire Dubh Sguadaig (*Corra Doo Skoo-atak*, meaning obscure) with its remote loch.

Moreover, Teallach enjoys an enviable location at the junction of the Great Glen and Glen Spean, giving it panoramic summit views.

Beinn Teallach has caused even more trouble for Munro's Tables over the years than Beinn a' Chaorainn. It wasn't even a Top before resurveying elevated it (just!) to the magic 3000ft mark in 1984.

Its status was ratified by a 2009 survey that re-measured its height as 914.60m (3000.8ft), since when it has replaced Ben Vane, re-measured at 915.76m (3004.6ft), as the lowest Munro of all.

Beinn Teallach from Roughburn (Glen Spean)
NN 377814, 8ml/13km, 690m/2250ft

Begin as for Beinn a' Chaorainn (Page 91): take the Roughburn forest track and branch left c.200m beyond the right-hand bend. Follow the track to the forest edge, where Teallach's southern slopes can be seen for the first time.

BEINN TEALLACH's confusing summit highpoints

Summit

Top of NE Ridge

Beyond the forest edge a path continues across a field to the Allt a' Chaorainn. Cross the river on flats below a small gorge to join a fairly good path along the far bank. Unless the river is low, it may require a water-splash or paddle.

The path climbs to join a boggy ATV track beside a forestry plantation. At the upper forest fence, when the track bears right to continue up the glen between Teallach and Chaorainn, climb straight up the hillside ahead on a more overgrown, even boggier track-cum-path. To call it wet is an understatement. Its line is not always obvious but it is worth following if at all possible. Leave it and you'll soon find out why – the gentle angle of the hillside has turned this side of the mountain into a vast marshy moor of clinging grass and heather.

As height is gained, the track gives increasing respite from the flanking terrain and eventually offers good walking as moor gives way to dry heath. As the angle eases even more, the track becomes lost on turf and boulders, but the going now is everywhere excellent as you approach the ▲summit .

Despite the squelchy ground, this can be a surprisingly pleasant descent route, with fine views of Loch Treig across Glen Spean to speed you homewards.

The map for this route is combined with that for Beinn a' Chaorainn on Page 92.

THE EASAINS

Loch Treig

Glen Spean

Descending from Beinn Teallach

▲**Creag Pitridh** 264 924m/3031ft (OS 42, NN 487814)
Craik Peetry, meaning obscure, possibly Petrie's Crag or from Gaelic
pit (farm) and *ridhe* (field), or perhaps a corruption of its name in the
original Tables: Creag Peathraich (*Craik Perrich*, Sisters' Crag)

▲**Geal Charn** 81 1049m/3442ft (OS 42, NN 504811)
Gyal Charn, White Cairn, probably named for its quartzite summit

GEAL CHARN   CREAG PITRIDH

Loch Laggan

The Ardverikie Trio is a compact triangle of Munros in the Ardverikie Forest on the south side of Loch Laggan. The forest is not a tree forest but a 'deer forest', as shooting estates were known in Victorian times, and no area of the Highlands is so richly endowed with stalkers' paths that give easy access to the heights.

Two of the Munros, as their names imply, are bulky mountains whose summit plateaus are encrusted with sharp quartzite rocks: Geal Charn and Beinn a' Chlachair (*Ben a Chlachir*, Mountain of the Stonemason).

Creag Pitridh, the third Munro, is a contrastingly conical little hillock that should consider itself very lucky indeed to be revelling in Munro status. From the bealach that separates it from Geal Charn, the elevation gain to the summit is a mere 105m/345ft. What was Sir Hugh thinking of?

Still, Pitridh's summit is a great viewpoint over Glen Spean, its flanks sport some beautiful crag and loch scenery... and it's one of the easiest ticks in the Central Highlands. For more effort, Geal Charn can be added to give a two-Munro outing.

Queen Victoria loved this area. She stayed at Ardverikie House in 1847 and considered purchasing it as a base (the present baronial building at NN 508876, seen across Loch Laggan from the A86, was built in 1877). However, the weather was 'dreadful' and the following year she fell in love with Balmoral. If the sun had shone that rainy August of 1847, perhaps Royal Deeside would now be Royal Lagganside.

Creag Pitridh from Glen Spean
NN 433831, 12ml/20km, 680m/2250ft

The route begins at the bridge over the River Spean just west of Moy Lodge, at the west end of Loch Laggan on the A86 (park in the lay-by beside the bridge). The first part of the trip is a 3ml/5km walk along Land Rover tracks to Lochan na h-Earba (*Lochan na Herba*, Lochan of the Roe). This is a 4ml/7km double loch (lochan?) that is hidden in a great trench behind the craggy lumps of Binnein Shuas (*Been-yan Hoo-as*, Upper Peak) and Binnein Shios (*Been-yan Hee-os*, Lower Peak).

CREAG PITRIDH

Sgurr an t-Saighdeir

Lochan na h-Earba

At a right-hand bend 300m after crossing the River Spean bridge, branch left on a track that crosses the moor and climbs to a T-junction beside a wood. Take the right branch here to contour around Binnein Shuas to a fork in front of a small reservoir. Take the left branch here to reach the sandy shores of Lochan na h-Earba at the foot of Creag Pitridh.

The elevation gain to the loch is only 100m/330ft, so a brisk walk should get you there in about an hour. In front of you the whole way are the northern slopes of Beinn a' Chlachair, indented by the deep scoop of Coire Mor Chlachair.

After crossing the bridge at Lochan na h-Earba's inflow stream, ignore the shortcut that goes straight on and stay on the main track, which curves right then back left, eventually to run along the far shore of the loch. After c.400m (cairn), branch right on a grassy track

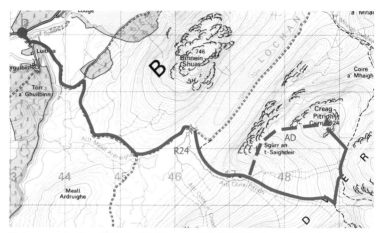

that crosses to the Allt Coire Pitridh, the stream that comes down Coire Pitridh from the bealach between Geal Charn and Beinn a' Chlachair (Bealach Leamhain, *Byalach Leh-an*, Elm Pass, named only on 1:25,000 OS map).

Once the track reaches the stream, it becomes a stalkers' path that climbs over the bealach to all points east and south. As far as the confluence with a stream that comes down from the left

(NN 473804), the path has been renovated so well that the surface gives even better walking than the approach track (really!).

Above the confluence the path becomes grassier but remains in excellent condition. At a fork just before the Bealach Leamhain take the left branch to climb around the foot of Geal Charn to the 819m/2686ft bealach between it and Creag Pitridh.

CREAG PITRIDH

GEAL CHARN

The stalkers' path above Lochan na h-Earba

From its highpoint, just right of the lowest point on the Geal Charn–Creag Pitridh bealach, the main path continues down the corrie on the far side to Lochan na h-Earba, while a baggers' path crosses the bealach laterally to climb each Munro.

The path up Creag Pitridh is indistinct at first but, after passing a small lochan, it becomes better defined and makes a beeline for the summit cairn up Pitridh's grassy eastern slopes.

At a final steepening, the path eases the angle by taking a dog-leg left and right. The ▲summit is an attractive rocky eyrie with a glorious view over Lochan na h-Earba and Loch Laggan to Creag Meagaidh, to say nothing of limitless views up and down the length of Glen Spean.

Alternative Descent: Sgurr an t-Saighdeir

The most effortless return route from Creag Pitridh's summit is by the route of ascent. For a more direct, more scenic but rougher descent to Lochan na h-Earba, go down the south-west ridge to the craggy outpost of Sgurr an t-Saighdeir (*Skoor an Sijer*, Peak of the Soldier) above the shore.

A path leaves the summit to head down the south-west ridge but it becomes intermittent. If you lose it, you may never find it again as the ridge becomes broader and more complex. You can continue all the way out to Sgurr an t-Saighdeir and descend from there around outcrops, but the going on the ridge-crest becomes so tussocky that you may well give up on the endeavour.

Left of the ridge, broad slopes of tussocky grass descend to the stalkers' path beside the Allt Coire Pitridh. If you fail to find a path down, aim for the stream's northern tributary, where you'll find a developing path along the bank. This joins the stalkers' path at the stream confluence, at the top of the resurfaced section.

If arriving back at Lochan na h-Earba on a sunny day you'll be faced with an extreme test of willpower – tearing yourself away from a sandy-shored sojourn for the 3ml/5km walk back to the roadside.

The balmy shores of Lochan na h-Earba

Bonus Munro: Geal Charn add-on return: 1½ml/2½km, 230m/750ft

GEAL CHARN

Although Geal Charn's summit is only 125m/411ft higher than Creag Pitridh's, the climb from the intervening bealach involves disproportionate effort. The convoluted 230m/755ft ascent, with the summit hidden from sight until the last moment, is a fair old climb.

The path is intermittent and hard to follow but the slopes of heath and rocks are climbable anywhere. Take a shallower diagonal line up than seems warranted, first along the edge of the corrie on the north side of the bealach, then up a complex hillside of bouldery knolls and grassy terraces that become rockier with height.

Eventually you'll reach the broad south-west ridge. Follow it across a minor rise to reach the large ▲summit cairn at its far end. If energy permits, take a stroll over the summit to the rim of the deep north-east corrie (Coire an Iubhair Mor, named only on OS 1:25,000 map), the mountain's finest feature of note.

GEAL CHARN

SW Ridge

Viewed from Creag Pitridh

▲**Creag Meagaidh** 30 1128m/3701ft (OS 34 or 42, NN 418875) Craik Meggy, possibly Crag of the Boggy Place
▲**Stob Poite Coire Ardair** 76 1054m/3459ft (OS 34 or 42, NN 428888) *Stop Potcha Corr Ardair*, Peak of the Pot of the High Corrie (the 'pot' being the bowl of the corrie)

CREAG MEAGAIDH

Coire Ardair

Loch Laggan

Creag Meagaidh rivals Ben Nevis as one of the great mountains of the Central Highlands. Deeply demarcated by glens to the north and Loch Laggan to the south, the massif of which it is the reigning peak boasts three Munros and seven Tops slung out along an undulating skyline.

The summit forms the hub of a Catherine Wheel of supporting ridges divided by corries. And what corries! Coire Ardair bows only to Coire Leis on Ben Nevis for scale and grandeur. Here, forming a soaring backdrop to lonely Lochan a' Choire, are nearly 2ml/3km of cliffs up to 450m/1500ft high, with towering buttresses split by great gullies (called *posts*). To add to its appeal, the corrie is tucked away at the end of a curving 4ml/6km glen that was specifically designed to hide it from the roadside.

Two other Munros, Stob Poite Coire Ardair and Carn Liath (*Carn Lee-a*, Grey Cairn), together with two intervening Tops, are found on the northern arm of the corrie/glen. The southern arm sports two more Tops and another three are dotted around the massif.

The walk up to the corrie is one of the great walks of the Central Highlands and it puts you within easy reach of Creag Meagaidh's summit.

Creag Meagaidh from Aberarder (Loch Laggan)
NN 483873, 12ml/19km, 900m/2950ft

The 4ml/6km path to Coire Ardair begins at Aberarder Farm car park on the A86 beside Loch Laggan. This path was at one time infamously boggy, but after Creag Meagaidh became an NNR it was improved dramatically using boardwalks made from railway sleepers. More recently still, the whole path has been upgraded to form a beautiful, well-gritted, perfectly formed, Alpine-style highway to the corrie – a textbook example of what can be achieved in the Highlands given the resources.

From the car park the path runs past the farm buildings and follows the glen of the Allt Coire Ardair all the way into the bowl of the corrie. It climbs the right-hand side of the curving glen well above the river, with an especially fine section that passes through the old birch wood of Coill a' Choire (*Culya Chorra*, Wood of the Corrie). Once around the bend of the glen, the great cliffs of Coire Ardair come into view and loom ever more impressively as the path approaches the imaginatively named Lochan a' Choire at its heart.

The route to the summit plateau traverses right beneath the cliffs to the curious nick in the skyline known as the Window (in Gaelic: Uinneag Coire Ardair, *Oonyak*). The renovated path ends abruptly at the far side of the lochan, leaving you with nothing but fond memories as you tackle the more customary boot-worn path that then continues up the hillside.

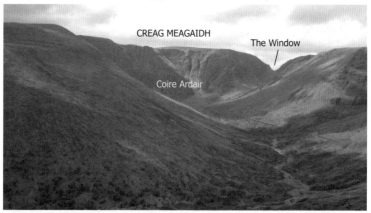

CREAG MEAGAIDH

The Window

Coire Ardair

In 1985 Creag Meagaidh was purchased for the nation by the Nature Conservancy Council (now Scottish Natural Heritage) to prevent it from being planted with conifers by the then owner. In 1986 it became a National Nature Reserve.

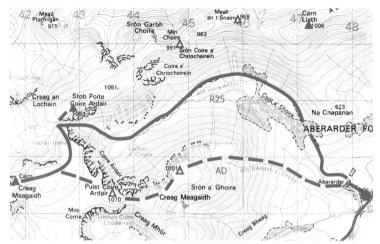

The path climbs through an Inner Corrie on grassy slopes to reach the foot of a boulder ruckle below the Window. A stony path climbs right of the boulders then traverses left into the Window itself – a bouldery defile between Creag Meagaidh and Stob Poite Coire Ardair.

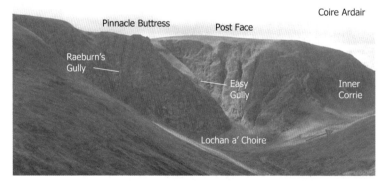

Coire Ardair

The shore of Lochan a' Choire is a fine spot from which to study the cliffs of Coire Ardair. The most awesome feature is Pinnacle Buttress, which rises like a shark's fin behind the lochan. To its left is Raeburn's Gully and to its right is Easy Gully (only easy by comparison).

Further right is the Post Face, riven by four vertical posts (gullies), and further right still, around the corner, is the Inner Corrie, through which you pass *en route* to the Window.

STOB POITE COIRE ARDAIR   Coire Ardair Northern Arm

Lochan a' Choire

Viewed from Coire Ardair Southern Arm

Turning left on the skyline, the path climbs a broad shoulder of grass and stones between the cliffs of Coire Ardair and the cliffs above Lochan Uaine (*Lochan Oo-an-ya*, Green Lochan), the largest of an attractive necklace of lochans on the north side of the mountain.

Finally, you arrive on Meagaidh's extensive summit plateau. Ahead on the skyline, on the side of a rise east of the summit, is the conspicuous large memorial cairn known as Mad Meg's Cairn. The smaller cairn that marks the ▲summit is on the rise just beyond, at the far end of the plateau.

Mad Meg's Cairn   CREAG MEAGAIDH

Lochan a' Choire

Lochan Uaine

The Window

STOB POITE COIRE ARDAIR

Coire Ardair's name is usually translated as High Corrie, but it is derived from the Gaelic *Ard Dhoire* (High Grove or Wood), perhaps referring to Coill a' Choire in the lower glen.

Bonus Munro: Stob Poite Coire Ardair
add-on return: 2ml/3km, 120m/400ft

From the Window the bagging of this nearby Munro is a facile but rewarding exercise. A stony path climbs easily along the northern rim of Coire Ardair to the ▲summit for aerial views over the abyss.

STOB POITE
COIRE ARDAIR

CREAG MEAGAIDH

Alternative Descent: Coire Ardair Southern Arm
1ml/1½km less mileage, 120m/400ft more ascent

The southern arm of Coire Ardair gives superb ridge walking with unrivalled views of the corrie. It even offers a shorter way back to Aberarder Farm. On the final descent you'll miss that approach path but, if you can handle some temporary rough ground, the rewards more than compensate.

From Creag Meagaidh's summit head south-east across the plateau on grassy terrain to the shallow dip at the southern corner of the corrie rim, below the rounded Top of ∆Puist Coire Ardair (*Poosht*, Post). The main path circumvents the very top of the Puist but it is worth going over the top for views down Raeburn's Gully, a classic winter climb that tops out just beyond.

Before continuing, it is also worth making a short detour south of the Puist to the rim of Coire Choille-rais (*Corra Chulya-rash*, Corrie of the Shrubwood). This has a perfect circular shape and boasts its own craggy lochan to mirror Coire Ardair's.

Beyond Raeburn's Gully the rim of Coire Ardair narrows and reaches Creag Mhor, a pointy cliff-edge peak (and former Top) that is the best-looking summit in the massif and which gives the best views of the corrie's crags and lochan. Beyond this lies a slightly lower twin pointy peak, then the ridge broadens. Slopes of rock-strewn grass descend to a saddle before a short rise to the flat Top of ∆Sron a' Choire (*Strawn a Chorra*, Nose of the Corrie).

Beyond Sron a' Choire, broad grassy slopes fan out towards a flat shoulder that marks the end of the ridge. Before reaching the shoulder, descend

Creag Mhor

Coire Ardair Southern Arm

Raeburn's Gully

Lochan a' Choire

Viewed from Stob Poite Coire Ardair

into the shallow corrie on the right, aiming for Aberarder Farm seen below.

On steeper slopes of grass and heather below the corrie, keep left, beside the leftmost streamlet, to find an increasingly worn path that makes a rough descent to the moor. If in doubt, you'll find the path lower down beside the main stream before it veers away left and passes a prominent boulder. The going is on the damp side but the path gets the job done.

On the flat moor it crosses an ATV track and makes a beeline for the Allt Coire Ardair, which it follows down to a bridge at NN 476874. The last section of path is becoming overgrown but remains relatively dry and allows easy progress. The dual carriageway of the ATV track is a tempting alternative but is wetter overall.

Both path and track lead to the bridge, beyond which the track gives the driest route to Aberarder Farm.

Sron a' Choire

On the Southern Arm   Creag Mhor

Sron a' Choire

Descent from the Southern Arm

INDEX

Descending from Ben Nevis

Luath Press Limited
committed to publishing well written books worth reading

LUATH PRESS takes its name from Robert Burns, whose little collie Luath (*Ga* swift or nimble) tripped up Jean Armour at a wedding and gave him the chance speak to the woman who was to be his wife and the abiding love of his life. Burns called one of 'The Twa Dogs' Luath after Cuchullin's hunting dog in Ossian's *Fingal*. Luath Press was established in 1981 in the heart of Burns country, and now resides a few steps up the road from Burns' first lodgings on Edinburgh's Royal Mile.
Luath offers you distinctive writing with a hint of unexpected pleasures.

Most bookshops in the UK, the US, Canada, Australia, New Zealand and parts of Europe either carry our books in stock or can order them for you. To order direct from us, please send a £sterling cheque, postal order, international money order or your credit card details (number, address of cardholder and expiry date) to us at the address below. Please add post and packing as follows: UK – £1.00 per delivery address; overseas surface mail – £2.50 per delivery address; overseas airmail – £3.50 for the first book to each delivery address, plus £1.00 for each additional book by airmail to the same address. If your order is a gift, we will happ enclose your card or message at no extra charge.

Luath Press Limited
543/2 Castlehill
The Royal Mile
Edinburgh EH1 2ND
Scotland
Telephone: 0131 225 4326 (24 hours)
Fax: 0131 225 4324
email: sales@luath.co.uk
Website: www.luath.co.uk